A CONTEMPORARY MEDITATION ON THE EVERYDAY GOD

A CONTEMPORARY MEDITATION ON THE EVERYDAY GOD

BY SALLY CUNNEEN

THE THOMAS MORE PRESS
Chicago, Illinois

ISBN 0-88347-061-6

CONTENTS

WHEN TOMORROW COMES...

When my father was four years old, playing on the floor, he remarked to his startled mother that "When tomorrow comes, today will be yesterday." Taking a minute or so to figure it out, she agreed with him. It has taken me all my life to realize not only the simple truth and the inevitability of his observation, but to catch glimpses of what this constant change means in human terms.

Such glimpses, as experienced during the past twelve months, will be the preoccupation of these pages. It has been a time for mulling over the multiple perspectives forced on me because of the passage of time. This June my youngest child looked at me sternly over breakfast as he was about to leave for camp and said, "You're acting like a mother again." This fall I decided that my teaching of English to adults in our community college was a permanent involvement and I started back to graduate school as a student of the philosophy of education. My age, my work, my relation to other people have all conspired to make this a true "middle" period in which I hope to integrate the intensely personal events in my own life with the larger social world of which I now know I am a part.

When I was very young, unlike my father, I had

no practical sense of time whatsoever and little interest in its progress. I felt both space and time were endless, and this sometimes posed dizzying problems as I gazed at the stars from the summer grass. Closer to home, of course, the demands of waking up and getting to school on time, keeping my uniform clean, doing my homework, all weighed so heavily on me I thought of freedom as escape to a relaxed emptiness.

Now in middle age it is clear that such escape from time and space is mere illusion. For space-time is the element I live in, as a fish in water. As a child I did not *know* it. I used to sing all the time in those days. I was in my element as I walked or biked or roller skated around the streets of Providence. But often my mind and body were quite dissociated. Only through the long process of growing and learning and friend-ship, marriage, motherhood, and the death of loved ones did I become intermittently but surely aware of my intimate entanglement with one particular and limited section of space and time. The change within myself from childhood to the present seems almost parallel to that from the primitive mode of life, in which one is at home in nature despite magical notions of its power, to the civilized, in which one is both semi-knowledge-able and alienated. Since I am divided, I no longer sing; instead I carry on a dialog with myself.

The saving realization that time has brought is that there *is* a self to talk to, not merely a part of the living forces around me. Every day brings questions that require me to relate the self to some past or present event or feeling. They tug at me like props and plots and characters begging me to pull them together. My conversations with myself in this book are my efforts to fuse these elements; fragments of childhood memories wil[1] alternate with current experiences and thoughts on recent reading. The project is hopelessly diffuse; the time strictly limited. But since that is our common human problem; I shall try to meditate in this year of triple-vision in the only way that seems possible to me: by looking attentively at His creation from where I stand.

THE NEED FOR A HUMAN SPIRITUALITY

When you decide to pick anything as ephemeral and subjective as the self to be your seeing eye on other things and events, there is an inevitable anxiety about the validity of your choice. It is helpful to hear a wise voice that unexpectedly confirms it and even provides a wider spiritual framework to support its fragility.

The voice I heard was that of Thomas Berry, Passionist priest and scholar in Eastern Religions, speaking last June at his Riverdale Center for Religious Research just north of Manhattan. This gentle man, one of thirteen children of a mother from the North Carolina hills, has a vision of spiritual needs and strengths today on a global scale that few can match in its daring assimilation of the conflicting signs around us. It grew slowly through the years as his traditional background in western history, philosophy and theology met and intermingled with the languages and philosophies of the great spiritual traditions of the East, then found manifestations of all these traditions flourishing in different groups and individuals here in the United States.

In his talk he made needed distinctions, but never lost sight of the main task we face today as the world's first conscious global citizens: "We must live in the totality of the human." By allowing our fears to cut us off from certain contacts with nature and others, we have in our time reached a crisis of energy symbolic of our overly rational Western approach to civilization since the Industrial Revolution. Today we need to listen to the earth itself if we are to be strong enough to learn how we can help it survive. The earth nourishes its offspring in the dark, secret places below, transforming decayed matter into life-giving nutrients. "What we need in Christianity today," then, Berry concludes with a disarming smile, "is more corruption."

All this may seem new and strange, but Berry says it is the reverse. Our oldest spiritual traditions, particularly those of interior piety, served precisely to relate the individual to the totality of the universe as microcosm. Today technology has placed us in the situation where we must reenvision our own traditions in conscious acknowledgment of the strivings of those in other traditions who are trying to do the same. We have in our lifetime discovered the total human system, there from the beginning, always acknowledged by religion, whose rituals functioned to make the member of a remote tribe feel *at one* with sky, sun and spirit. Spirituality must be called on today to produce the same effect in very different circumstances. Our rockets, airships and interplanetary communications systems force us—who do not understand *ourselves*—to realize that our problems are soluble only on a world level. Religion as we have known it must seek deeper roots if it is to address itself to the task of forming world people.

But what can we do in Hoboken or Cincinnati about becoming world people? Berry believes it is precisely as individual human selves that we must begin to reexperience the sacred. Only in the person can humanity, cosmos and history become present to one another. It is *here* that we must work in the immediate future if we are to develop a spirituality that answers our own needs and talks to the hunger of others. Each of us must regress deeply into our inner selves and encounter the numinous (or holy) as well as the corruption within us. I will revisit my own childhood and go even further back to my grandmother's, for only in this way can I see my own social origins and feel again the birth of my emotions. Roots are necessary for any top growth. In the past, holy men and women did this digging for the rest of us; today we must *each* do it if we are to help build the world community that seems so necessary but is otherwise so impossible of attainment.

It does no good for us as Westerners to try to move into a timeless "Eastern" mentality and attempt to stay there, except perhaps in brief pauses, for the sake of individual sanity, for the pressures of our Western time are moving inevitably round the globe. We must learn to deal with our space-time where we are, calling on inner resources which we have hitherto ignored— caught up as we are in getting and spending and repairing; or escaping for the long weekend.

Things don't happen all at once. There are signs around us. Not always visible, particularly in the churches. But I notice among many young people a growing enjoyment of and respect for their bodies, and an eagerness to use them as a disciplined means of expression—in dancing, acrobatics, yoga, even in their fascination with more nutritious food and delicious ways of preparing it they are more respectful both of the body and the earth. The land that produces food is seen as a limited, living gift, so that many third and fourth generation sons and daughters of European immigrants today share with the native-Americans a feeling of awe and responsibility for the land that nourishes them. Through the scripture of their own being they come to read the Creator's power.

This is a part of what Berry means by regression; he believes that as we reexperience human dependence on the natural universe we also find a rebirth of human freedom and dignity. Our imaginative powers are called on, we respect our own experience as we learn the awesome task of being the psychic dimension of the evolving earth process. I feel the earth under my feet here in West Nyack—hot, dry, prickly today, and realize it is the same earth the Indians walked when they named Nyack (point of land) and forked that ancient oak (the tree specialist tells me) to mark a trail. The evening news says that this air they breathed is now threatened not only by pollution but by global ozone loss.

Berry's talk about recovering our childhood so that we could see our present with new strength and vision seems much less self-indulgent than I feared. He has recaptured a large part of the earth's cultural experience to share with us: he speaks with great sensitivity of the Chinese approach, which has always mingled feeling and aesthetic response with the intellectual. He appreciates the Chinese virtue of authenticity, *Ch'eng,* that ground of all other virtues implying inner sensitivity to the heaven-given being within so that one, through dialectic, can recover one's "last" early identity and see its connection with the total human community as well as the cosmic and divine order. He insists on the Chinese insertion of the human, as it achieves self-transformation, into the trinity of powers (with earth and heaven) as able to transform others. The powerful person in China, then, must keep self-hidden, must be reticent and withdraw, must *not* become a professional holy man. We must each, accordingly, be our own medium in this groping towards a deeper spirituality. Berry's rich cultural message translates into our biblical background as well. Study the prophet Jeremiah, Berry advises, and you will find the Lord delivers much the same message to him: "Brace yourself, Jeremiah. . . . This day I make you a fortified city, a pillar of iron, a wall of bronze, to stand fast against the whole land . . . for I am with you and will keep you safe."

THE TIME GAME

I pushed myself against all my biological inclinations to get to the garage early for the necessary car overhaul. With all deliberate delay I arrived guiltily one hour late to find that the promised tires—to be put on at the time of the overhaul—had not arrived.

I felt lighter, more alive, as I swung the car out, promising close contact by telephone so that we could pounce on the wandering tires when they arrived. Driving to the post office, I observed the green-orange hills, gently mounding on either side behind the usual roadside necessities. I felt the springs of choice arise within me. First I went to the cleaners to see if they had been able to clean the ink stain on Joe's new suit. It was almost invisible. Next door to find Paul's boots reborn through the shoemaker's ingenious patching and resoling, yet with those old Karmic lines that bespoke their earlier incarnation.

As I turned to the swinging post office door, steeled to face the bureaucratic questioning of the postage on my packages, I became aware quite suddenly of the nature of the game I was so enjoying. Stall time. Put off something scheduled. Have a whole day to feel free in.

Meetings cancelled, snow days, even friends who were coming to dinner and can't, all have the effect of renewing hope. They exhilarate me. Yet I know, just as I did entering the post office, that I am playing a game with time. I sense time as a shadowy opponent in this encounter. Perhaps a little like the knight playing chess with death in Ingmar Bergman's *The Seventh Seal.* My game is not ominous now. But I think, as I emerge from the not unpleasant ordeal of adding stamps to *Cross Currents* packages, that it is essentially the same game the knight played. Why, then, do I so much enjoy breathing in the crisp fall air and pondering: what shall I do next?

* * *

I have begun reading a wise and challenging book, *In Parables,* by John Dominic Crossan, (Harper & Row, 1973) that relates what Jesus was trying to tell us in the parables about time. Most of the stories deal in actions with triple rhythms, Crossan finds: someone finds something, sells something, buys something else. What Jesus said to the rich young man seems to summarize the point: Go, sell all you have and follow me. Hard words—disruptive. Yes, says Crossan, the message of Jesus has often been misinterpreted. He was not illustrating timeless truths or proclaiming the Kingdom "later," using the parables as colored, moving pictures to illustrate the talk. He was speaking about the *present*—the moment in which He heard the word of the Lord. He found that word to be deeper and more powerful than any social or legal or religious law, and for Him it shattered all those other words. And so in trying to express the Lord's power, He turned instead to the natural imagery with which the parables are filled, for these forces of time and nature represent the inevitable surprise and chance that disrupts our carefully planned future.

Surely this relates to my attitude at not being able to get the car done: the unexpected surprise, the delight. It is the power of spirit I sense in this present—I feel the potentiality and it gives me joy. I am not yet fully attentive, I know, nor ready to sell all I have. But I believe I have at least begun to hear what the parable is saying. It is not about seeds or storms or trees, but it is also not about finding "the church" or even Himself as a resting place, as I thought earlier. These parables speak indirectly, as they must, to our own present, in which they say: Open your eyes to what is around *you* and see it in a new way. Pay attention to the power of our Mother-Father's creation, for it is calling on you to give a response just as it did on me.

The "free" time Jesus had was one in which the surprise of God's word released Him from the usual social constraints into a much more demanding service. Seeing the power of the present, he was able to checkmate His shadowy opponent. I have only just become aware of the true nature of the game.

A PENCIL DRAWING

Brushing my hair I look out the window at the brown leaves on the bright green grass. The outline of the trees begins to show again through the remaining leaves against the gray, clear sky, and I feel a surge of possibility despite a debilitating series of fall colds. Remember, I tell myself, that not all things are possible; just a few, so choose the first one carefully.

Inexplicably a diagram comes to my mind, blotting out the view—a simple pencil drawing Pat Keegan had made at a small party in London in the summer of '49. The peppery leader of the English Young Christian Workers, who was to be one of the few lay observers at Vatican II, was trying to show a group of us Catholic graduate students how his concept of God had changed during and just after the second World War. While we ate potato salad, he drew a small circle on a pad, talking energetically in the kind of accent we wouldn't hear much in the states till movies like *Room at the Top,* workingman's English, neither cockney nor Oxford. He drew other circles away from the first one, then straight lines between them.

"Now we all know that God made us and put us in one spot here," he said, pointing to the first circle. "That's our family in our home, and that's where He expects us to start work. I've come a long way from the personal encounter with the Infinite I used to think of as a religious attitude." He pointed to the other circles: "That's where we do our religious creation, right here on the job, with the people we meet in the homes, pubs and shops we're in."

It hit me even then with the power of truth, though the idea of all the baptized being called on to incarnate the message of Christ in what was a unified sacred-secular universe seemed at the time almost an underground message from the Church. It would be some time before what Gregory Baum referred to as the Blondelian shift, crediting French Catholic philosopher Maurice Blondel with the emphasis on the unity of one's life and work with one's religious vocation— would become a major one in the Catholic church.

Keegan's attitude seemed so sound and crucial it stimulated me to search for other voices to develop it. Many of these (including Blondel) would appear in the pages of *Cross Currents,* then a-borning, started in large part to show that there need be no intrinsic split between faith and intellect, church and world.

But the drawing had also aroused personal memories. Growing up in Providence, I had walked on the lines between my own circles of school and home, library and church, and felt the inner tension that came from *not* seeing the religious task there. My best friend Peggy and I were getting A's in school, acting in plays, spending our days debating and bowling and, in general achieving at Classical High School, but we both were in love with the Catholic faith. And it seemed to call for something exotically different and heroic. We would visit churches and pray silently after school and on the weekends. Our Lents were orgies of self-denial. Peggy persuaded me to give up lipstick for Lent when I was a junior and even to give up ice cream at the dancing-school party, and it was only later I found out I had persuaded her that it was more sacrificial *not* to give them up, since it was so obvious to everyone, and since we so much wanted to. I was not sure what kind of heroism our faith ultimately demanded as I abjured C movies, avoided meat and said not a single word on Good Friday. But when Peggy decided to enter a cloistered Carmelite order and I knew I would not be talking to her anymore, I had a sharp sense of separation and pain, compounded by a feeling that I did not agree with her confession to me that she could *not* live as a Catholic in "the world."

I had yet another crisis, wondering if those lines between those simple circles could ever hold all the dedication and emotion faith seemed to demand. The complications of work in New York and a disappointed love drove me, too, to think of the (to me) unwelcome possibility of a simpler life in the convent. Since it might, after all, be the "better part," I arranged an interview with a likeable Sister who ran the local parochial school.

She spoke movingly about prayer and service, and I began to warm up to a sharing of concerns. Suddenly, seeing my sympathetic response, she revealed her innermost feelings: "Don't you think that things are so bad in the world of today that anyone who really cares about Christ is better off out of it?" I felt suffocated; an indistinct "no" was all I could muster. But if ever I made a specific decision as to vocation, it was at this point where I chose not to abandon "world" no matter what the contradictions that seemed to keep it so tragically separated from "Church".

Until today I had never related Pat Keegan's drawing to that interview; strange that the pencilled diagram should recur to me twenty-five years later as I brush my hair in rising hope of living one day well. Shall I merge with the motion of the wind in the brittle leaves? Talk or sing with Paul? The uncompromising diagram reminds me that I am more circumscribed than I might choose to think. I must look more closely at the circles in which I move and understand myself better so as to choose well which lines I'll take today and why. Not too much calculation, of course; the process gets more instinctive as you get older and learn your limits. You know too that eternity can come in a minute and you can take it—then still go on afterwards to another circle by another line, perhaps making a slightly different arrangement when you get there.

Our conscious relation to our own space-time is surely the essential geography and economy we need as Einstein and Keegan both knew. Both insisted on this relativity which puts the burden of choice on me as I stop brushing my hair and look once more at the day outside. But the mental digression has been healing, for I no longer move in a vacuum, but as part of a living world that is choosing and creating itself all around me. I think I'll go brush my teeth and join it.

TRUE LOVE

Bland music fills the small room as I sit in the dentist's chair awaiting my final cleaning operation. "I give to you and you give to me," I sing under my breath to the slow orchestrated tune, and in the background of my mind I hear the Original Bing Crosby-Grace Kelly duet. "And on and on it will always be. True love. True love." The dentist is picking and probing, but I hardly notice. Exaggerated slowness and many instruments give the tune, slight at best, almost the sound of a parody. Was Cole Porter doing here what he had done with "Wunderbar" in *Kiss Me, Kate?*—making fun of the upbeat love-duet in the middle-brow musical? Heavy with violins, the score rolls around the dentist and me as he whirrs away the plaque with bubblegum-flavored sandpaper.

"For you and I have a guardian angel on high with nothing to do." The audacity of the thought disturbs me now as it did when I first heard it. What a distortion of the sacred in service of the saccharine profane! "But to give to me and to give to you love forever true." Banal, but perhaps with some truth in that, given the right interpretation. The silent couple conclude the refrain in my mind with the utmost sincerity: "Love forever true."

Porter could never have written such drivel straight. Why then, as the dentist mercifully says, "Rinse now," am I still tingling with a satisfying and almost total belief? Simple sentimentality wins out over my better judgment almost every time. It is wise to remember how easily I melt into the perfect sucker.

YIELDING TO TEMPTATION

Like Saint Francis of Assisi, Emily Dickinson got drunk on sun and flowers. Leaving the damp November outside I enter the darkened library stacks and sit down in the carrel facing the seductions that await the intellect. Before me lies a book-lover's smorgasbord: a volume of Flannery O'Connor's *Wise Blood* is carelessly topped by Edwin O'Connor's *Edge of Sadness.*

Since I am here to do research on the Boston Irish of my grandmother's youth the latter intrigues me, yet I could hardly choose between him and Flannery, who lures and baffles me by her sharp vision, its moral acuity embodied in bright sharp physical detail and conversation.

But just underneath in this stack is a faded volume of Alcott, and on the shelf above a large book invites me with the title *Roger Williams: The Church and the State.* Temptations of the mind—promises of meeting historical figures and wandering with them through the past—they are so much more powerful at pulling one away from present duties than the temptations of the flesh. They offer rewards that last, that begin to connect with one another and that one can keep. (Luckily I had a good bowl of soup and a sandwich at *Chock Full of Nuts* so I do not have to test the comparative lure of food. I have always been drawn to those artists and authors who felt food and culture were inextricably related, such as Virginia Woolf, Willa Cather and W. H. Auden.) But is this great desire to consume the ideas and imaginings of others in print not the kind of spiritual temptation Faust himself gave in to? It was not, however, power over natural things he wished; it was illusion, super-powers, the opposite of true knowledge of the human situation.

My Catholic guilt cannot last long before this feast. I plunge into the poetry of John Boyle O'Reilly, fascinating Irish rebel who became editor of the *Boston Pilot* in 1876, and saw the connection between the Negro's cause and that of the Irish. Then I delve into police records, settlement house reports and William Shannon's suggestive history of the Irish in America. The appetite doesn't give out as it does with eating or drinking, just the time. There are so many avenues worth taking—too many—perhaps in time this mental prospect will pall in its promise of satisfaction as food did for me the first time my parents took me to a superb buffet at the Bath and Tennis Club. What did it matter that the lobster newburg, the shrimp curry and chocolate mousse could tempt, since *I* felt stuffed and could hold no more? Clearly, physical satisfactions lacked something. But in the library I not only stuff myself, I can take more home with me, and in time the helpings begin to merge with other thoughts, stories and experiences.

Driving back under dark skies, I am reminded that when my schedule kept me home without that buffer space of imagined intercourse with the ideas and stories of others, I myself seemed to become an object. One thing among others to be kept clean and running. This thought had come to me the previous week when I had flown to Indiana for an unexpected opportunity to chair a workshop on world hunger. Alone in my room after acting as "facilitator" at a few strenuous meetings, I found I took good care of myself within the short time allotted for rest, then lost myself completely in the absorbing task of seeing that everyone said what they meant and wanted to say, and that we could also come to some consensus and common action. At home in the same time-span I would have done little. A good deal of the difference, therefore, lies in what you are asked to do. Yet I must have greatly limited what I asked myself to do—even thought of myself as being able to do.

Taking this same drive home from class in Manhatten earlier this winter with a friend who is also taking courses, I had heard her talk about her fierce personal need to do something with and for other people outside the home. Many of her neighbors seemed to live for acquisitions, and in this atmosphere she felt "wiped out". Learning to be skillful in working with children who needed remedial help in their speech she came alive again. Connie's urge is to help others; mine just to wallow in finding out and sharing. Connie also told me a story of a friend of hers with two children whose husband was so successful that their home was a museum of period furniture, bone china and oil paintings. The friend was becoming increasingly tense and insecure there, feeling inferior to the things among which she lived.

Perhaps the temptation in the library should be indulged; surely it would help Connie's friend to build up her own inner forces somewhat. I'll read a story as soon as I get home. Dinner may be somewhat late, but lost in Flannery O'Connor's world (I feel strong enough tonight for one of her self-revealing tales) I know I will later be filled with enough energy to make it up to the hungry souls who need it. They, too, are hungry for more than food. So, filled with the rightness of Mary, instead of the righteousness of Martha, as I pull into the driveway, I turn off the engine, enter the house and head for the bookshelf.

FAMILY TREES, ROOTS AND A HIGH VIEW

We need to listen to the earth, said Tom Berry. We need to recover our past and our childhood if we are to become strong and flexible enough to help create a present that has a future. For me these goals united in a personal search into the past, triggered by reading about attempts by school reformers like Horance Mann and Henry Barnard to heal class gulfs in New England in the latter half of the nineteenth century, to expose underprivileged children to "the habitual practise of cleanliness, delicacy, refinement, good temper, gentleness, kindness, justice and truth."

I had Irish-American ancestors on the receiving end of these reforms, and yet I knew almost nothing of their experience. I knew only one schoolday's incident about my maternal grandmother, Gaga to us, who had attended parochial school in Boston in the 1870's. As a widow she lived with my opera-singing aunt, Geraldine, whose cheerful, ebullient temperament matched her own. Geraldine told me the story: One day when the Christmas season approached, the question arose as to how Jesus and Mary reached Bethlehem. Gaga was quick to respond. "On an ass," said the young doctor's daughter matter-of-factly. The teacher seemed unaccountably embarrassed and prompted, "It was a donkey, wasn't it?" "It was an *ass*," repeated my grandmother, even though she had to wear the dunce cap for the rest of the day. Years after hearing this story, I was delighted to find her stubborn faithfulness confirmed by biblical scholars who ordinarily use the distinguishing terms "camel-nomad" and "ass-nomad."

But this was a legend of a uniquely powerful personality, a young woman who convinced a whole theater party later that she was the new Irish maid, sneaking out for the evening in her mistress' clothes. Stories about Gaga who seemed always to transcend her surroundings, could provide no context for her life in the community. Mere fragments of disconnected names and incidents relating to this Boston background came through to me as a child, and these were puzzling. Geraldine's stories were happy and funny: about Gaga playing the piano every time the mailman came down the street because she wanted people to know they were the first Irish Catholic family there to have a piano. My mother's stories were sad, about constant confirmations from society of inferiority, and this made no sense to me. Nor did she wish any connection with an Irish background, which her occasional comments linked with vulgarity. She and my father were modern, secular Americans, well-dressed, avid theater-goers and suspicious of the social clannishness of our local parish. They believed in tolerance and progress.

I thought of myself as an *American* Catholic. Gorging myself on English stories from King Arthur's and Robin Hood's time on down, I felt no real break in my fantasied cultural evolution from Magna Carta to the 300th celebration of the founding of Providence in 1936. When my mother's unaccountable humiliation broke through—as it did in her reaction to Eleanor Roosevelt, with whom she worked in the Al Smith campaign (my mother found her condescending) I thought my mother peculiar. Nor did I understand the force of her emotional attachment to Joseph Kennedy as a symbol. Gaga had encouraged young Joe Kennedy; family legend has it she told him, "Joe, you can do anything you want!" But although my mother had known both Rose and Joe, they had never been close in taste or interest. I found it embarrassing that she would clip pictures of the Kennedys from the paper and pin them up. I began to resent this smiling, successful family at an early age. Only when I was about to go to college and both my parents warned me about the bigotry and pain I would suffer in the New England women's college I had chosen did I sense, briefly, some connection between these odd likes and dislikes and living wounds in their own lives they had never before revealed to me.

But I was rushing away to college, work and then marriage. I lost both my parents and Gaga before my first child was born, and Gaga and Geraldine—who had seemed timeless visitors of summer, clattering up to our house in an ancient Chevrolet full of children, games and music—had joined each other in Holyhood Cemetery before I had the time to ask them all the questions about their childhood I now wanted so much to know.

For as an adult, with a greater sense of how individuals and social groups interact, I felt that the gaps in my own knowledge of my forebears prevented me from passing on necessary information to my own children. Darkness and confusion about my own Boston Irish roots cut me off from knowing what place I occupied in the social landscape today. All the discussions I might have had with the main characters, trying to make some kind of coherent design out of our separate time-strands of American experience were now impossible. Seeing if I could find connections to take myself back through the maze was the underground purpose of my hours in the dark riches of the library.

From history books, old newspapers and records, a context began to grow in which my small questions dissolved and larger ones emerged. I found out about the tragedy that had been communal life in Boston in the latter half of the nineteenth century. Forced by the arbitrary actions of British landlords to evacuate their land in the late 1840's, thousands of penniless Irish immigrants, their families disrupted, sailed to a Boston they were too poor to leave. And Boston at that time was so far beyond the American Revolution that it tended to think of England as the mother country.

The geography of the city was such that all of these newcomers would be huddled together into crowded, unsanitary slums. Its economics would use them as cheap, over-worked "hands" in unsafe factories and as domestic help. Thus built-in-segregation and demeaning roles would determine the vision native Bostonians would have of them, even as many of the newcomers involuntarily antagonized these citizens by going on the welfare rolls.

The long settled Boston families whose sons went to Harvard lived in another world culturally, spiritually and physically. They dutifully endowed universities, founded the Museum of Fine Arts, the Symphony Orchestra and the Opera House. They supported charitable foundations like the Perkins Institute for the Blind, and were less exclusively interested in acquiring wealth than their counterparts in New York or Chicago. Yet

into this London of the New World had come a
group of people who would feel this very culture
and benevolence as oppressive.

One final uniquely Bostonian attribute would
make the clash exquisitely bitter: its moral tone.
Bronson Alcott had called the city the purest in
America. Despite good Brahmin intentions to aid
them, consequently, an often unconscious pre-
judice and condesencion would come through. A
brief report from the Captain of the Boston Night
Watch on a raid in the Irish section in 1858 con-
veys in capsule form what this might mean to
immigrants of a different culture and morality
seeking to escape their crowded tenements and
fifteen-hour workdays. "One hundred sixty-five
persons had been arrested," Captain Savage
recorded, "for the various crimes of piping,
fiddling, dancing, drinking and all their atten-
dant vices."

My original question about school reform in
Massachusetts at this time had been apt. The
Irish community believed that a good deal of such
reform was instituted to take away what little
control they had over education in the neighborhoods. Mann's requests for funds to encourage
"prompt obedience" and "self-control" among
students could only be understood as criticism of
their homes. That pure Boston morality pervaded
the language of reformer Henry Barnard, too,

when he urged that young people be removed as early and as long as possible "from the examples of rude manners, impure and profane language, and the vicious habits of low-bred idleness, which abound in certain sections."

Based on such ignorance of themselves and of the alien immigrants, the reformers' hopes of overcoming social spilts in the schools would inevitably be dashed. Many Irish never went to school at all, and those who did attended schools where the majority were Irish, so a healing social mixture never developed. Meanwhile, the predominance of Irish in these city schools increased the desire of many native Bostonians to move to the suburbs so that their children could be educated with "other American youth," away from the unpleasant "odors" of the Irish.

Two separate, unequal and antagonistic cultures lived thus side by side in Boston in the latter half of the nineteenth century. Almost complete cultural separatism followed the residential and economic segregation. The obvious institutions set up by Bostonians to help or care for the Irish were psychologically resisted. When one learns that Catholic chaplains did not earn the right to serve in state institutions in Massachusetts until 1879, one sees at least some reason for the Irish suspicion that they were being proselytized in these hospitals and prisons. In any case, they did not want "to be beholden" to the charity of Bostonians, and they set up their own charitable and cultural societies, thumbing their noses at their benefactors. In saloons and on the streets the Irish would slowly learn how to build a political organization that would take over power in the city by the end of the century. It is enlightening to read in Van Wyck Brooks' *New England: Indian Summer* how this development was seen by those who had represented that region's earlier "flowering." "The Boston mind appeared to have lost its force," Brooks suggested. "It was yielding, inch by inch, to the Catholic Irish." (N.Y., Dutton, 1950, p. 422). The Irish entered the power vacuum high-minded Bostonians had left them, and would now improve their economic and social position. It is worth noting, too, that John Ireland, the liberal Archbishop of St. Paul, perhaps showed more social wisdom than greed in his famous remark that it was the responsibility of American Catholics at this time to become millionaires.

Ironically, when a few "made it," in Archbishop Ireland's terms, and began to direct their fate somewhat, they took the path the Boston Brahmins had trod long before. Joseph Kennedy, for example, like a true nineteenth century Bostonian, deliberately prepared his sons for public service and his daughters for lives devoted to culture and charity. Taking on the role of American Ambassador to England was an important symbolic gesture, helping many Irish-Americans to heal old wounds of inferiority and separateness from the wider American community.

All this was the wider picture whose details the library helped me fill out, and from it I learned that my family had been among those who escaped earliest and lightest from this Boston tragedy. Yet I could see why my mother had ambivalent feelings, felt still ashamed of a tradition of poverty and disease over which she had no control. I understood why Gaga wanted to show off her piano to the mailman.

My research in the library had been multiply rewarded. Now I felt a warm sense of identification with the Irish-Americans who had come over here in conditions of deracination comparable to that of the African slaves. I was furious at the injustice that forced them into crowded, unsanitary, ugly hovels and then blamed them for being there. Having received a more realistic conception of my background than the one I had concocted as a child, I could now understand and sympathize with my parents' desire to put it all behind them. Dealing with its effects had caused them so much pain the best they could do was try to be whole human beings regardless, and this they did admirably.

They could hardly be expected to achieve and communicate a dispassionate social commentary on what their parents and grandparents had experienced. But this perspective was just what time had given me, higher up on the family tree. Feeling at last a living union with my ancestral roots, I was also able to see this microcosm of social history in Boston a hundred years ago as a true tragedy, not just a good-guy, bad-guy scenario. The native Bostonians had erred from ignorance and good intentions, and the Irish had flaunted their differences in the face of the benevolent, blue-nosed natives. Human nature is recalcitrant. Until the Irish felt respected, they were not free to act according to their best ideals of behavior. I think it is essential for us today to grasp the complex processes that enable an individual or a group to move towards the ability to choose how one acts. To see how one must move from powerlessness to power to freedom to choose is more than ever important now when we see so many groups of different cultures, native and foreign, facing the same need in this country today the Irish did in the nineteenth century: to overcome slights, inferiority, and economic deprivation so that they can affirm their own dignity and join in honestly in what is still an American society to be created.

One last view: Looking down at the function of

the Church among the Irish immigrants from my present perch, I can see more clearly the vastly different position it occupied then and now. The Irish in Boston had not exactly chosen their Catholicism—they were fused to it like Gaga to her rosary beads in old age.

For us, their descendants, reacting against both the institutional separatism and the later illusion of secularism which denied difference, the Church is no longer a powerful unquestioned force shaping and preserving our identity in an alien land. It is itself torn between ideas and groups who embody the same differences that split apart the Irish from the older Bostonians; we have our own self-realizing Emersonians and our own unbending purists.

Can we separate what has given us identity (our past, our physical, psychological and social present) from what we want to be committed to (our future)? If we do, are we not split in half, sell-outs, Irish who made it and became Yankees? Even saying it so bluntly I know the question is muddy. In many ways they were neither free before nor after; many did not have a choice. But if we cannot choose to relate these two demands today, how can there ever be a human community that can bridge the exacerbating grievances that feed self-hatred and violence to children and grandchildren?

Today, in all its seeming disarray, the Church may have a positive, healing answer to give to this crucial question. It can and should affirm our identity, even as it preaches the Incarnation, as it did for the Irish. But to be *Catholic,* it must affirm all other socio-ethnic identities as well, even those beyond my capacity to know or understand. That is the meaning of the symbolism of communion. It is not a separate "pure" event. Like human history it is obviously physical, not just in its form but in the life outside the church to which it promises unity. The Eucharist cannot be a comfort to me except insofar as it is also a challenge, reminding me how much imagination and suffering are needed to live with and for all those blacks and Asians and southerners and poor folk, not to mention the sinners, among us all. It is this call for unity with which we are sent out after each mass.

Naive goodwill is not enough; neither is physical charity, as the Boston experience proves. What is needed is a much more patient and thorough understanding of the intricate processes of human development—including self-deception and institutional bias—so that the Church does not find itself impotently calling for "peaceful" attitudes or "unselfishness" to groups of people who are not humanly free enough to make such moves. Virtues are exercised when people have fought the difficult battles that give them the *power* to be peaceful or unselfish. Instead, the Church today, and each of us, might show compassionate understanding of all human struggles for freer choice, even as it holds out, too, the ideal beyond the clashes that best encourages growth towards that full humanity we see in Jesus, who exercised his power in choosing to be powerless.

GOD IS EITHER A FEMINIST...

When I was twelve I had a most unusual and totally inexplicable experience. At the time it seemed simple and healing. Now, I wonder.

Eighth grade was my last in St. Sebastian's, fortress of order, bastion of obedience, champion of clean uniforms. Mother Grace was the marshal of this tight little island, where we marched in rows according to height in and out of ancient classrooms and halls brightened by the faces of deceased local bishops, regularly sending our teachers off for hushed-up nervous breakdowns. We learned to parse sentences inside out, built cribs and made blankets for the baby Jesus with our tireless ejaculations. We competed lustily for gold stars and grades, for every month the aged pastor would come in and read off all the names in the class in order of performance as he handed out report cards.

But eighth grade meant the end of this sheltered existence. I had already picked Classical High School but I knew that, too, was only a way-station. Going every Tuesday night to the Novena of Our Lady of Perpetual Help, I had learned that each of us must choose a "vocation." Gathered together before the semi-magical blue and gold Byzantine painting, the group of suppliants sought to ask the Blessed Mother's help for their most important intentions. The priest passed out cards with a list of ten possibilities; we were to check one and place it in the box near the picture. Looking down the row, I could find nothing quite suitable: neither "return to health," "for a loved one," or "grace of a happy death" appealed to me. "Vocation" seemed foreign, too, but having discovered by asking its meaning that I would have to choose my course in life, I suppose I became unconsciously concerned about that momentous decision in my mysterious future.

It was then that we began to talk in class about what we might like to do when we were grown up. Most of the boys wanted to be doctors or lawyers or reporters; the girls wanted to be nurses or mothers or secretaries, which seemed dull and depressing to me. I had *no idea* what I might want to be except Anne of Green Gables in our class play. We were all trying out for the different parts then, and conscience gave way to desire as I did not put my heart into the test for tight-lipped old Marilla but gave heroine Anne everything I had. I had read the book at least four times and found Anne's zanily imaginative approach to life most sympathetic. I won the coveted part; my mother made a beautiful white organdy dress with puffed sleeves for me to wear in the last scene, and for several months I was more Anne than myself.

But I knew underneath that couldn't last

either, and one Tuesday night I finally checked off the blank after "Vocation" and placed it in the box under Our Lady's picture. A few days later I slipped into the darkened church on my way home from school. Alone among the oak benches, I sat quietly for a while about half-way toward the altar, watching the flicker of the red sanctuary lamp. Daylight still filtered in the stained glass window above the altar, and Mary and the apostles gathered around Jesus in vibrant color.

I had not known quite why I had come, but suddenly emotion seized and I fell to my knees. "Oh please," I begged silently, "When I am grown up, let me be a cowgirl!" I suppose I had been building up to it all along, seeing Gary Cooper movies, reading Zane Grey, but only at that moment did I realize just how much I longed for all that open space in my future life.

After an interval of silence, I seemed to hear a voice talking to me calmly and softly. I was sure it was God. The voice said merely, "If, when you are grown up, you want to be a cowgirl, you will be a cowgirl." This response did not terrify me in the least, nor did it disappoint me. I felt deeply reassured, left the church, and never mentioned the incident to anyone.

Now it intrigues me. Is God a feminist, or just the best diplomat in the universe?

DOUBLE-VISION
ON THE LAND

Travelling west to Notre Dame on Route 80, heading for Fr. Jack Egan's summer program in Urban Ministry where Joe and I will each give a workshop, I find myself seeing the green hills and neat homes in varying perspectives. Whizzing by farmhouses tucked in the rolling Pennsylvania landscape, I am aware that behind the domestication, primitive land exists. Mists cluster low round dark uninhabited mountains, and the red sun sets large, unobstructed by anything human. And even as the Pittsburgh Pirates announcer calls over the car radio for a large contingent of the "babushka league" to show up at Forbes Field on Ladies Day to root for the home team, an uneasy feeling of what it might be like to stand alone on that dark hill outside comes over me.

Barefoot on that hill, for example, I would not see the pretty purple-pink flowers that border Highway 80 and cover even most of the tawny rock. I would be far more aware of animal and insect noises, of brambles and the cold, hard surface of the rock I had clambered up, fearful of snakes. But now I could breathe freely, arms extended wide to embrace the fiery sun, a deep physical thrill intensifying my interior response to the majestic end of day in all its power to suggest my place in the universe: minute, but a living, knowing part.

When the children were younger I had crossed this same land imagining what it might be like to live in this stone farmhouse or that small white eighteenth century townhouse. It is impossible to know, of course, for the feeling of a place can only be grasped when you live there and experience the force of the social field invisible to the scanning eye. Such make-believe is great fun unless someone takes it seriously; then it becomes an immediate burden: so much lawn to cut, unquestionably the ragweed count is too high here, too far from the ocean, and who wants to go through the tedious business of selling, buying and moving!

But this kind of unreality is nothing compared to the accepted pattern of life in the motel we stop at for the sake of the pool's cool exercise. All air-conditioned and carpeted, ice-cubes constantly reforming in whirring bins down every hall, too much soap, too many towels, shades drawn, the blank TV tube calling for attention. Is there an energy shortage? We may create one but we certainly won't acknowledge it. Is there really land under the motel? Bushes and animals outside? As the rock band reverberates over the air conditioner's hum, it is hard to realize that we are on a hill that has recently experienced sunset.

I am merely the latest visitor from the East to have such double vision while moving across over endless highways. Although I cannot fathom what goes on behind the sunglasses of fellow travelers as they shop for souvenirs at truck stops, the theme of moving West has been a familiar one in American literature. Two famous examples of going back in time as a retreat from Eastern corruption and a return to heartland simplicity occur in F. Scott Fitzgerald's *The Great Gatsby* and Willa Cather's *My Antonia*. Superficially, the desires and attitudes of the two narrators resemble each other, but examined more closely, particularly in the meaning they ascribe to the American landscape, they are almost as different as a motel and an Indian cave-dwelling.

Recall the last page of *Gatsby*. Nick, betrayed by Tom and Daisy's ruthless use of wealth and power to maintain their miserable but secure position, stands on the shore where Gatsby had stood, staring across the harbor at Daisy's green light, the inevitable victim of his—and our— American illusion that success could insure the dream of happiness.

Disgusted now with New York, knowing the parties are over, Nick is leaving for the mid-West next day. Handbags packed, he stands on the beach, and as the moon rises he sees the houses melt away until they reveal the virgin land the Dutch sailors once saw, "a fresh green breast of the new world."

For the last time in human history, Fitzgerald writes, man had a hope, a high dream, a possibility equal to the human capacity to wonder. Gatsby had still sought that dream long after the trees the Dutchman saw had vanished to make room for his house. He did not know, Nick mused, that "it was already behind him, somewhere in that vast obscurity beyond the city, where the dark fields of the republic rolled on under the night."

Gatsby had believed in the future, Nick comments, and so do we, not realizing that we are pushing against the current, our boats "borne back ceaselessly into the past." The image is beautiful and nostalgic, but the emotion is one of frustrated self-pity. The land so hauntingly evoked is not respected nor is the past; only the dreams of the Dutch sailors are invoked, for example, with no hint that these might conflict with those of earlier inhabitants who had kept that world green.

In Willa Cather's ending to *My Antonia,* Jim Burden revisits the scene of his happy childhood on the Nebraska prairie, similarly disappointed with life in the money-getting East and his own marriage. Seeing his childhood companion Antonia flourishing on the rich land he had left, he discovers "what a little circle man's experience is." The very road he is taking had carried Antonia and him to events and accidents that would determine all they later became. "Now I understood that the same road was to bring us together again. Whatever we had missed, we possessed together the precious, the incommunicable past."

To see the difference between these attitudes, we have to go back in Cather's novel and see its meaning in the narrator's life. In a fictional introduction, Cather says she met Jim Burden on a train going back over the wheat fields to Nebraska, and that from their "observation car," they saw the dust, heat and wind which recalled their childhood and especially a Bohemian girl they had both known. "More than any other person we remembered, this girl seemed to mean to us the country, the conditions, the whole adventure of our childhood. . . . Jim had found her again after long years."

The novel recounts Jim's childhood (which greatly resembles Cather's own) so that we may learn what he has recovered. As an orphan of ten he comes to his grandparents' home and discovers wild, untamed land: "I felt motion in the landscape; in the fresh, easy-blowing morning wind, and in the earth itself, as if the shaggy grass were a sort of loose hide, and underneath it herds of wild buffalo were galloping, galloping." He also sensed an absence there, for it was "nothing but land: not a country at all, but the material out of which countries were made."

When Jim is first left alone on the land after taking a walk with his grandmother, he experiences a moment of complete happiness through fusion with his surroundings: "I was something that lay under the sun and felt it, like the pumpkins, and I did not want to be anything more. I was entirely happy." It was noteworthy that the lines that follow were engraved on Cather's own tombstone: "Perhaps we feel like that when we die and become part of something entire, whether it is sun and air, or goodness and knowledge. At any rate, that is happiness; to be dissolved into something complete and great."

Shortly afterwards, however, he meets the young Antonia, eager to learn the language he can teach her, and able to teach him, as she matures, how to tame that land for human habitation and happiness. Although she is a believable character, particularly as a young girl, Antonia is also clearly a mythical figure. Just as the Nebraska plain recalls the flat cornlands of Eleusis, so does Antonia embody the civilizing role of Demeter, goddess of the grain, and this interpretation of her role solves what have been puzzling questions about her relationship to Jim, why a male narrator was necessary, and why the story has such a strange power over us.

From the beginning, with Antonia a few years older than Jim, the reader is warned that the relation is not the usual romantic one. Yet there is intimacy and Jim's confession to her sons that he always loved their mother. In the story, the intimacy and understanding breaks down when Jim does not comprehend Antonia's working on the land like a man. He moves to the small town of Black Hawk, and though they are again re-united in friendship when Antonia is hired for a time by the family next door, Antonia keeps young Jim at a distance. She insists, for example, that the lovely Lena Lingard not distract him from his studies. Before Jim is to leave for the University, he has an outing with Antonia and the other hired girls in which they all share a vision central to the book's meaning.

Jim and Antonia talk together while the other girls swim, and for the first time Jim reveals to her the compelling experience he had had of her dead father's presence. Like Jim, Antonia believes with great happiness that he has gone back to the woods and fields of home that he so loved.

The old friends are as one. They share a sense of union with the spirits of the dead and of the sacredness of places associated with them. The other girls now join them under an oak tree, and add a series of praises for the endurance of their mothers under impossible suffering. These details are of the pioneers' lives, yet they also parallel the substance of the myths surrounding Demeter. This passage is revealing because it warns us not to see Antonia as a simple fertility symbol. Several of the other girls will use their wits and craft in serving their choice *not* to have children, as Cather did herself. Tony *chooses* her life. Strength of will as well as choice are inherent in Cather's version of fertility. It implies a realistic knowledge of self and society in which one is faithful to a life that one continually creates. This element of choice and of creation should not be forgotten in the ripe vegetative and physical fruitfulness of Antonia's garden at the novel's end.

With the group still gathered under the oak tree by the river, Antonia persuades Jim to tell them how, when he was younger, he and Charley Harling had actually seen a stirrup and sword dug up by a local farmer that proved Coronado had come this far north in search of the seven golden cities, before he "died in the wilderness of a broken heart." Just then, a curious sight appeared to all of them. As the red sun rested on the high field against the horizon, the black figure of a plow stood out in dark relief against it. "Magnified across the distance by the horizontal light, it stood out against the sun, was exactly contained within the circle of the disk; the handles, the tongue, the share—black against the molten red. There it was, heroic in size, a picture writing on the sun."

This central image ties together all the book's themes. Coming as it does during this close spiritual union of Jim with Antonia and the other hired girls, it suggests the wisdom of that union. Following directly the story of Coronado's failed quest, it suggests the reason for that failure. Only in working the land, not in trying to plunder it, can man find happiness—the kind Jim had experienced in the pumpkin patch. In Cather's experience the plundering oil and coal millionaires had won out, but she still saw an alternative. It was one that required a closer and more creative relationship between the individual, his place and his way of living. Demeter, let us recall, was helped by the Sun to find her daughter's whereabouts, and to learn the mystery of rebirth herself. Demeter was also the goddess of civilization, and the presence of the different immigrant girls as well as Jim stresses the pluralistic and communitarian nature of Cather's vision.

Jim and Antonia part ways soon after this scene; he to a way of life that leaves the soil and to a marriage that is childless. Antonia will be seduced, abandoned with an infant, and then have all returned in abundance, a pattern reminding us of Demeter. Antonia's acceptance of death, betrayal and hard work are rewarded in the glorious burst of fruitfulness that greets the middle-aged Jim who returns from the East, a little scared that she might have changed. The "veritable explosion" of life he finds there made him dizzy for a moment. His fears prove groundless; her identity is unchanged. "Whatever else had gone, Antonia had not lost the fire of life." In Antonia's triply enclosed orchard, he experiences the "deepest peace." It is like the peace he had experienced in the pumpkin patch, but it is one that had been won in human terms through a lifetime of work. It recalls, too, the image of the plough against the sun. Coming back to his own childhood, Jim finds a vision of continuity that will now relate him to Antonia's children. As Demeter suggested continuity in an uninterrupted sequence of births, so too does Antonia, whom we recall Cather and the fictional Jim Burden associated with the country itself, hold forth a promise of proliferating American life, if we can return to her wise teachings and example.

The fictional Jim, then, returns to Antonia just as he is about to enter that last critical stage of human development, that in which one reassesses one's life and prepares for death. Unlike Nick, whose disillusion with the Eastern money-getting he shares, Jim finds something to come back to.

In Jungian terms, Antonia is Jim's own Anima. It is particularly fitting that Cather should have chosen a male narrator, not only because the anima is traditionally feminine but because it is precisely the traditionally feminine in cultural and religious terms that Jim, the typical American, has turned his back on as he pursued the industrialization and the undermining of craftsmanship and human dignity that followed. The "feminine" side of our national psyche has been repressed since our break with the Amerindian past. These are feminine mysteries in the archetypal sense that Cather gives us, and consequently her past is a timeless space, one that is a living source of psychic change.

Some sixty years after Cather wrote this novel in the face of her own disillusion, I think we are better prepared to understand the healing vision she has given us. Each time I reread *My Antonia* I am astonished at both its simplicity and its living power to suggest who we, as Americans, are, and might still be. Unlike Fitzgerald, Cather says it's not too late.

*   *   *

Still on Highway 80, flat green plains of Ohio and Indiana, still the layers of civilization—gas stations, motels—but every so often the mythic corn and the silver, restorative water.

DREAMS

This year—by chance?—I am taking a course I wish I'd had long ago: Human Growth and Development, the attempt to study life's cycles and the questions of identity and relationship they pose. On the first day the psychoanalyst-teacher asked us to keep a journal throughout the term in which we would put down our reactions to the discussion and reading. He said to pay particular attention to matters that disturbed us or excited us, for such affective responses were always significant. He also suggested we try to see the relation between our present reactions and the material we were dealing with, which was mainly concerned with early childhood development.

Perhaps I'm like my father. As a young man he wanted to study medicine, but was dissuaded by a physician friend who told him, "Newman, you'd *have* every disease as you studied the symptoms!" Well, the night after being told to keep the journal, paying particular attention to dreams and affective responses, I had my most vivid dream in months.

Falling asleep over Josiah Royce's theory of the Social Infinite, I dreamed I was in the country house in Rhode Island we'd gone to summers when I was an adolescent. All night long I seemed to be undergoing scrutiny by the curious country folk amazed at how late these new city people got up and how strangely they behaved. I felt uncomfortable at their prying and dismayed by the verdict of the farmer's daughter that we were "rich." I certainly didn't feel rich (as I had not years ago when these events occurred) but merely embarrassed and I was glad to wake up. Yet I was puzzled by this inappropriate dream.

Making coffee I asked myself, since I should have to say something sensible in the journal, could Royce's book have any connection with my dream? I have often found last influences at night to be significant. I tried to summarize what I had been reading. The idealist American philosopher had been arguing that we need a *third,* an interpreter, i.e. other people, to help us know ourselves. I choked on my coffee; my unconscious had grasped the lesson before my conscious mind and summoned up a classic instance of such mediation from my own unsorted experience. Compared to the children in that country village I *was* rich, but blocked by my own adolescent sense of awkward, insecure identity, my vision was not clear enough to see what would have been apparent to the cold eye of an observer. My summer friends were telling me something I should have known yet could only really take in years later.

All right, so Royce's theory made sense to me. Now I was even more interested in the process that led me to that conviction. Normally, had not the psychology professor asked me to pay particular attention, I would have shaken off the dream and gone about my morning's business—called the plumber, corrected papers. Even if it had hung on, a strange haze over breakfast, the relation between the raw material of the dream and the theory simmering on one back burner in my mind would not have been apparent to me except for the translation into the generalized language I felt obliged to give it for the journal's sake. Summarized, the connection with Royce's theory was unmistakable.

What extraordinary complexity the human psychic organism reveals. One tends not to notice its subtle messages, its creative responses. How ironic that I should need a graduate school professor to tell me to pay attention to myself. It is embarrassing to admit that I never before fully realized just how critical and sensitive one's whole self can be. But results are never automatic; we can ignore, misinterpret or even refuse to act on this complex data we receive. Active intelligence as well as will is involved in responding.

Furthermore, the presence of the past including its emotions, in intimate connection with present problems, astonished me. Approaching the unconscious forces within me with some awe—those powers one read about in Freud and

Jung and hesitantly acknowledged—it had never before occurred to me that they might work not only to reveal deep desires and psychic flaws but also to serve as a kind of experiential computer, delivering data from the memory bank to aid in the pursuit of knowledge. We scarcely realize what amazing creatures we are. We need others to help us find out; then we must work constantly to evaluate and integrate what we learn into our understanding and our behavior. Willa Cather's plough against the sun is just as illuminating a symbol for this process as it was for the direction Antonia and the country should take. The creation of the world is still going on; our invitations to participate seem to have been delivered in our very psychic structures.

A few months later, my courses over and now pursuing a heavy reading schedule in philosophy, I woke up unaccountably in the middle of the night questioning my analysis of the previous dream. I felt disturbed at the possibility that I had imposed my interpretation on the dream. Perhaps the memory from adolescence had occurred for totally different reasons than those I slapped on to them for my journal's sake. But why, I asked myself sitting up in the dark, should such doubts occur to me months later, in the middle of the night? Recalling my previous method, I remembered that I had been reading a commentary on David Hume, the eighteenth century Scottish philosopher who questioned closely the assumption that because one thing preceded another it necessarily had any causal connection with it.

Lightning again. This time my unconscious had come up with an instance in which I had made just such a judgment as Hume had questioned— believing that because my dream occurred after reading about the need for others to mediate reality to us, it necessarily stemmed from that reading and ideas associated with it. Under Hume's close questioning, my unconscious felt troubled and summoned up the former dream for reconsideration. The example was so perfectly appropriate to Hume's doubts that for me this was evidence enough the reading did call up the dream. Researchers at MIT would need more cases: I am convinced that the present, waking mind summons up in some mysterious fashion the relevant memory within, whether or not we are consciously able to see the connection. Paying close attention is our responsibility. And I must be careful what I read late at night. Obviously I'm just like my father.

*   *   *

Speculation on these dreams has led me to recall the English class I taught the day after the first one. Conveniently, I recorded a few details in the journal. The group in this introduction to literature consisted of some 29 middle-aged students, the majority women out of school at least 10 years. Most of them feel strange at first with one another; they come from ethnic groups that might not mingle except here in the community college classroom. They have children, they work, yet something they feel they have missed sends many of them here.

We had read Katherine Mansfield's "Miss Brill," the painful story of an imaginative old woman's realization that she is a lonely figure of fun to others. As I asked for reactions from the class, I was struck with the external, physical orientation of the comments. One young girl replied to my question, "What happened?" by saying, "Nothing happened. It was all in her mind and feelings." "Is that nothing?" I continued. "Nothing *real,*" she replied.

Later on that day we considered the nature of figurative language. I asked the class to consider the following couplet:

> Joy and temperance and repose
> Slam the door on the doctor's nose.

One student insisted this was a literal statement, while another said it contained no metaphor because it was not about any real things. I began to sense that some of these people came to class with a sense of self that was largely material. The powerful social forces that treat us like mechanical beings have been successful in making us see ourselves that way: You are what you own, or how you look (being what you eat would already be an improvement towards a more organic conception).

There in front of me were people who seemed to think of themselves as physical, social things. Yet I knew from other classes that they would be intrigued by extra-sensory perception, hypnotism, mind control, reincarnation and many other manifestations of an occult or exotic nature. The glimpse I had had today of the limited, socially induced sense of self in some of them could well be a clue to this fascination. Something inside them might well cry out: This is not reality; this is not what you are.

I came to two conclusions after this disturbing revelation in class. The first is that because they see no connection between their interest in occult matters and their own sense of self, their perception of life and literature is distorted. Because their intellectual notion of themselves is split off from their desire for exciting, spirit-filled as well as critical personal response as part of their daily mode of living, their perceptions of reality are equally split: familiar physical things, unexplicable occult forces.

The second is that this perception can be altered. A teacher had helped me discover subtle spaces where my thoughts and feelings interconnected with ideas, just by asking me to pay attention. Why can't I do the same thing in my class? Ask my students to observe closely the way their feelings relate to the events in their lives. Perhaps this kind of intermediary focus on helping students connect the fragments of their feeling and experience with their thoughts is one of the few ways a teacher might lead them to educate themselves.

SECOND-STAGE MOTHER

"Will you take me over to the highway, Mom?" the twenty-one-year-old son asks, giving away no information.

You are in a bad position here, being the mother. You can't ask where he's going without seeming to be prying. He's too old and experienced for you to warn him about the dangers of hitchhiking; he knows a lot more about that than you do. There is no reason to refuse.

So he gets the pack and the canteen he takes everywhere, and you get your pocketbook and start out to the car. Trivial conversation about the slowness of the motor's pickup tells you that his mind is off in other places, impatient to leave physically. You are the mother. There is no way to talk to him as the interesting, particular man you already see him becoming with others.

"Over there's all right," he says authoritatively but somewhat grimly, opens the car door, scarcely looks at you and slams it with a formal, "Thanks. See you later." You sit there overcome with conflicting emotion (which he has to get away from, naturally) as he climbs down the hill on the side of the entrance ramp to the four-lane highway roaring with continuous traffic.

He is gone into the rushing mechanical impersonality of the road. You have no control whatsoever of what he will do or what might happen to him. All communication is cut. You could pray, and you do, briefly, before starting the car, that the unknown citizens on whom you must now rely for your son's well-being will be kind, responsible.

This is the second stage of motherhood, the one you were not prepared for. Hard enough to take the first one of total and seemingly endless care, understanding, reassurance, band-aids, ear-aches, teacher troubles, continual change in problems and relations. Then to have to turn it all off; equally necessary. But the emotions have been trained; in a different way care becomes a bad habit. We all know this. It is why people make jokes about mothers; they are always offering us chicken soup and rubbers when we are concerned about our lives, our loves and our eternal souls. But who else is asked to reverse roles completely in the same job?

Being a good mother seems impossible to me. At best it is a compromise, and more difficult when it is your main concern. Then your emotions are too involved, and your identity; you find it even harder to turn them off when your child is grown, when he looks at you and says, "Take me to the highway." And you do.

MISTAKES

Thinking back upon times when I have failed other people, I recall two instances in particular revealing the traps I made for myself that led me to diminish the lively spark in others.

The first occasion was a long hot drive through heavy traffic to an industrial area in northern Jersey where I was to pick up some boxes of envelopes for the magazine. I lost my way among the unfamiliar streets where old ethnic neighborhoods punctuated the aged brick factories. Finally, somewhat disturbed, I asked an old man strolling how I might get to the warehouse. Leaning in the window, he smiled a little and said that would cost me a quarter.

I was so flustered I believed him. Yet the gracious style with which he turned to me should have been unmistakable. He was glad I had asked him, happy to be able to tell me, and graceful with a heritage of playful gentility towards the opposite sex. But all this I thought of later as I ruefully followed the accurate directions he gave me. Seeing I misunderstood, his face had sobered. Both of us were used to others really demanding money, and I had been too quick to expect it of him, not sensitive or trusting enough to let him reveal his kindness at his own pace, in his own joking way. I had missed my chance to play that game with him. Now I wait a little longer before I jump.

The other instance is even more illuminating because it occurred precisely through my intention to do the right thing. Anna is a friend of my mother's who is quite alone now and increasingly limited in her activities. I feel responsible, yet am often frustrated by her abruptly negative replies. "Do you want anything at the store?" I often ask, or "Would you like to take a ride?" The answer is almost always a sharp remonstrance. "No, there's nothing I want. It's much too hot—or too cold— to take a ride." Both of us feel annoyed after these encounters.

One day my old friend Dorothy came to visit Anna with me. On the way she stopped at the drug store and asked me if there was any candy Anna liked, and I recalled she liked some coconut bars. Dorothy gave them to her; Anna seemed pleased, and the two of them began to talk about my mother and the old days when we were children. Just before it was time to leave, after a very relaxed visit, Dorothy turned to Anna and said. "Ellen wants us all to come to tea. Here, you put on your sweater and we'll have you back in an hour and a half. She especially mentioned you."

I waited for the snappy retort and saw only a grateful smile. I followed the two of them out to the car. Dorothy was beschmeigling her. Did I

really approve of that? Wasn't she being sneaky,
not helping her to see that she should learn to
make her own choices and not be flattered into
things? On the other hand, Anna was happy and
having a lovely time all through the tea, talking to
the children and eating cake. I have always
believed that people should do things they want
and not be forced or manipulated into them.
These were the rules I had been applying in my
approaches to Anna. I had to admit they were
quite unsuccessful. The behavioral psychologists
could have told me as much. *Don't* force people to
change consciously by asking their opinion. Any
parent should know this is an open invitation to
an argument. If I had paid attention to Anna
instead of my rules of fair play I would have seen
that she had a horror of choosing. The trick was
to find out and do the thing that pleased her as if
it were the most natural thing in the world.

To do this wasn't hard. It just meant going
against my own principles. I realized that it was
not only good psychology, it was the message of
Jesus the Pharisees found so hard to take. No
amount of following rules and becoming perfect
will work if you do not pay attention to the particular person and situation that confronts you.
My own pharisaism had been blocking me from
doing the right thing, from actually applying that

splendid advice in my favorite prayer of St. Francis: to seek more to understand than to be understood. Perhaps a little more sneakiness is necessary for real Christianity.

THE SHAPE OF THE UNITY
WE SEEK

(—Wild word visions written during interminable discussions on the topic in an ecumenical group that would never choose one.)

If we are to think of shapes, let us at least throw out anything flat. Something organic would seem to be appropriate, for it suggests growth as well as purpose. Since we are including the human and social aspects of our hoped-for unity, however, we need something quite vast and complex, perhaps a form of the solar system: independent bodies moving around a sun which attracts and regulates, nourishes and warms. If we could then imagine all of this moving harmoniously and cooperatively through time-space by two means (and I ask you to make the difficult effort to keep both ends of this metaphor in view throughout): *communication* of a clear kind, understanding of a high order and *passing over* (either through understanding, empathy or actual travel). If we can I think we might manage to maintain the organic connection we need to remind us that human beings as well as the Church are rooted in this world, evolving, at one with the historical universe. It would also help us remember that better communication with all other groups is a means to create that unity in motion that aims at eventual harmonious convergence. It would by its nature also remind us that centering is essential to each body as it moves with the others, and each would feel free, therefore, to operate from its own historical traditions. Such a moving vision of our hopes would give us a present impetus to realize that work strengthening any of these or other bodies around personal centers, thereby increasing their ability to choose responsibility for others, is already working towards our goal.

My other suggestion for a shape, equally organic, is more artistic than the astronomical one. It is that of a complex mandala, circles with centers within squares within a circle. This vision of the flames of consciousness comprehended by a circle also reveals our need for separate centeredness. It comprehends many levels of awareness, different directions and layers, yet all within a healing whole. Each human center as suggested by figures within the whole has its own time-space locus, yet the impulse of the total figure is towards integration. Mandalas are traditional in all cultures and abound in nature itself; hence they are meaningful in terms of depth psychology as well as religion. Although they stress the local "now" and include conflict, they reveal that all this is a part of wholeness.

Either of these shapes would suit the aims we

have as we hope for unity. They both suggest separate individuals and groups, seeking deeper centering within themselves, but all upheld within a powerful divine Spirit by whom they are attracted or all-encompassed. Both allow great independence at the local level, but in the mandala this might be shown by bright lights at each place of conscious, spiritual force. Large clusters of bright lights might indicate churches, but there should also be small flames for any individuals or larger ones for any groups seeking to develop persons, for this spiritual illumination is possible only in persons. Lesser lights of all kinds could turn, as part of the processive pattern, shake hands or dance with dark and horned creatures with ugly faces, in the awareness that the development of light centers will shift through this process of conflict if the ultimate harmony is to be that of the spheres.

I conceive of our organized religions as larger objects with influences of light able to encourage and support the other strivers with a good conscience and a forceful tolerance. Let a hundred flowers bloom and let us fertilize them, confident that the Spirit is using us in the process. Such images of Christianity seem to me to add just the touch of corruption Berry believes it needs.

THE UNEXPECTED IMPORTANCE
OF THUMBSUCKING

Perhaps my stage of life, which gives me a rich fund of memory and lures me on to the life of thought, tends to make physical reality less weighty (provided, of course, one has enough to eat). A tendency develops to forget the importance of the body and the absolute dependence we have on it. Certainly I found it hard to take straight the continued insistence of the psychologists I read for the course on human development on the importance of bodily functions for the child. From my lofty adult point of view these children who loved to play with their feces or were scared silly of castration seemed improbable.

My mind could assent to the epigenetic principle—each stage of organic and psychological growth must be gone through in its proper time sequence successfully before one can reach the next stage, or else there will be distortion and malfunction in the mature organism. Oral and anal stages were theoretically true for "children". But for myself? My journal reminded me that I exhibit irrational tendencies to eat when I am disturbed and to bite my nails under stress—obvious vestiges of unresolved oral problems. I could, however, see no reason for such behavior except the weakness of my will, since my parents had always made me feel loved and wanted, showering me with food and time and things, yet not to such an excess as to spoil me.

Yet men like Erikson, who seemed both wise and informed, insisted, for example, on the vital importance of thumbsucking. I had ambivalent feelings reading D. W. Winnicott, the English analyst, who insisted that sucking the thumb was a natural and comforting transition from the breast, sometimes reverted to regressively by anxious older children. Slowly my memory was jogged, sparked, I believe, by a very detailed passage in Winnicott's *Playing and Reality* describing different styles of thumbsucking. I recalled the different methods my sister and I had employed when we were children. I still harbored feelings of shame as I remembered my style: sucking the right thumb meditatively as I moved slowly from left to right of the blanket with the binding between the thumb and index finger of my left hand. I cannot recall when it started, but it was quite early. I remember later being intrigued by my younger sister's quite different method of placing the two middle fingers of her hand in her mouth, the index finger straight up by the side of the nose and the thumb sticking out perpendicularly. When we were older (me 10 and she 7 or 8) I used to police her thumbsucking for my parents at the Shirley Temple movies we were allowed to see.

Different as our styles may have been, I see now that thumbsucking gave us much in common. Because of the vigorous and unstinting action of our parents to eradicate the habit, however, I did not then feel any bond. Though I cannot remember at what age it was, I still remember my intense disappointment at being deprived of blankets with a binding. My dynamic method of thumbsucking depended on the smooth, cool binding which covered the otherwise rough blanket. When I was older and had the nice blankets back, I again reverted to thumbsucking and this time my vigilant mother used some bitter aloes on my fingers, and, when that failed, she tightly fastened metal casings over hands and fingers. I remember my sister was treated in the same way. By this time we had a younger brother to cope with.

I can see now that I had undoubtedly been disturbed by the birth of my younger sister. I remember hearing her scream in the next room when I was about three. My Mother rushed in and I thought what a nuisance and intrusion this baby was. My Mother's attempts to explain her to me or enlist my affection for her failed utterly. All through childhood I nursed psychological resistance to her and occasionally burst into violent, though largely symbolic, acts against her when I felt she had gone just too far.

I am still struggling to relate to this sister; last

night I dreamed of her and found myself again in the role of being both disgusted with her and, from my superior position of understanding and self-control, kindly suggesting to her ways in which she might redeem her situation. Although we were both adults in the dream, we were living in the house in which we lived as children, and the messiness she displayed then—dirty clothes all over the house, no sense of personal possessions—was transferred to her adult behavior as a mother. Pondering on the possible connection of this dream with my waking concentration on thumbsucking, I began to see that her birth must have made me very insecure, and that I turned to thumbsucking then as a comforting mechanism. When my parents insisted on depriving me of that comfort, my anxiety and doubts about my position were increased and I projected all my annoyance at my parents onto my younger sister. When, two years later, a little brother appeared, undoubtedly we both had the same reactions, and both reverted to the thumbsucking I recall at the later stage. Only now do I remember that my mother had two miscarriages after that, was quite ill and away at the hospital for some time. One of our funny family stories about my younger sister was her bold announcement to my mother in the hospital bed that she should "get up off that bed and go down town and buy me some new clothes!"

As I think back on these events, I believe it is clear to me for the first time that all the annoyance I felt at my mother was conveniently aimed at one target I felt as a threat, but only a small one. Thus I was able to achieve two goals: first, I could continue to love my mother and believe that mother loved me. How could I as a child of three afford *not* to believe my mother meant it when she took me in her arms each morning and told me I was wonderful? Second, I could then be sweet and pleasing to my parents so as to gain more of their affection by proving myself superior to this primitive creature that had invaded my kingdom. No wonder I have had serious problems working out my relationship to this sister!

But there appears to be even a deeper dimension to the prohibition of thumbsucking in terms of my own identity and ability to relate to reality which may also account for some of my sister's problems in coping with me and with her own reality. I am now convinced that D. W. Winnicott is correct in the importance he assigns to elaborate ritual thumbsucking as a transitional stage between the breast and the outer world in which the child's imagination builds its images of reality. When it is accompanied by movement along a blanket, as it was with me, thumbsucking is more than auto-erotic comforting; it is an important part of the child's move from autonomous self-gratification towards a working relationship with other objects and people. It is a stage between the imperialistic infant and the objective adult. In my case, the process was disrupted. I remember no special object that replaced the blanket in my affection. I did not have dolls or toys I loved. I turned, rather, at a very early age (5) to reading for the kind of gratification I had sought earlier in thumbsucking. And the kind of reading I took to was myth and fairy tale. I lived in world of fantasy from which I did not easily emerge. None of the games of the children around us (in which I often joined) appealed to me nearly as much as my books, and I left them with great reluctance. I wonder now, for example, if the serious accident I had in a ball game at age 8 when I had been prevailed on to leave *A Dog of Flanders* was totally accidental!

Although I cannot be sure, I suspect a break occurred in my development between the physical and mental that became a serious problem in my search for identity as well as in my understanding of what was real. I lived more in King Arthur's court than in my own house, and my immersion in books further separated me from my younger sister who read nothing but comic books. Now I suspect she had a reason for *not* reading, and lately she is making up for it. I became "the smart one," she the "pretty" and "athletic" one. In retrospect, I think we were more alike than not. In our common anxiety, which might eventually have brought us together, we unconsciously turned against each other. I have no idea what difference it would have made if we had been allowed to suck our thumbs in peace, but I suspect it might have helped us allay our fears and possibly to relate at least a little better to one another. Our search for pleasure was wrenched and distorted, and we took paths that would lead us into deep antagonism.

Only now do I see how my sister resented me, though, being small, she sometimes showed her feelings in overadulation, taking my things and trying to share my friends. When she was about two-and-a-half, she wandered from the summer house (where I was supposed to be watching her) and "ran away," telling the friendly ladies who picked her up and gave her lollipops that she had no parents, only a *mean, older* sister who beat her. Until this moment I treated this story as a funny one, never sensing the connection between her predicament and my own. Never realizing that her sense of imagination, which I thought on the despicable Bugs Bunny level, was in every way the equal of mine and a lot more in touch with her real situation.

In our family we did not repress our feelings; we tended to express them all too loudly. My reasonable father was heard to complain that he lived with Irish fishwives and asked us why we couldn't be civilized like the Jewish family next door. I suppose all this expression kept me from some problems, but it certainly did not add to my understanding of the feelings expressed. Nor did it alleviate all anxieties. As a girl, I had many nervous rituals including hair-pulling, foot-tapping and stepping on all sidewalk cracks. Reading was clearly my escape, but it exacted a cost. I felt myself different from other children, did not relate to them easily, and had to wait a long time before I could find a special friend who liked the same kind of imaginative play-acting I did.

In fact I had trouble telling fantasy from reality. I remember once having read in the *National Geographic* how the mail was delivered in one African country by men who would swim across rivers holding the letters over their heads in tin cans. The stamps were exceedingly rare and valued by collectors round the world. I was about ten and collected stamps then, largely at my father's prompting and with his active help. A week or two after reading the story I told some children of a friend of my father's that I had one of the tin can stamps. Of course they found out I did not and accused me of lying. I was stunned when they said I lied; it had never occurred to me as lying. I felt I did have the stamp even though I knew I did not.

Not being sure of the boundary line between fantasy and reality was quite painful to me at the time of my first confession, for it appeared mandatory to have something important to say. For months in my own mind I dwelt on an earlier transgression: at age three or four I had disobediently stolen out of the house during a nap to see a beached shark that was the talk of the community. I magnified my disobedience into a sin that seemed worthy of capital punishment. The guilt was real and very destructive to an ego not certain of its own reliability.

It is hard to be sure, of course, where imagination itself ended and where reading stirred up my own fantasy. I believe, however, that the reading was related to the needs served earlier by thumbsucking. The connection with food is clear enough, for even now I greatly enjoy eating alone, especially when I am reading, and feel strangely ashamed if someone else is present and not eating. At any rate, the early forced break in my life between a physical and a mental way of seeking comfort seemed to make it extra difficult for me to see the unbroken connection between matter and spirit. Although I have been able in recent years to rebuild and reenvision such connections, and am now eager to learn scientific information I scorned as "materialistic" years ago, it is only in this musing on my own childhood that I am forced to admit that something as childish as thumbsucking can be very important. I do not, of course, say anything so simple as "All my problems would have been solved if my parents, beyond loving and caring for me, had let me suck my thumb in peace until I stopped of my own accord." Yet I cannot help but see a real connection between that interference and certain ambivalences I have had in my view of the world, in sources of pleasure, and in a tendency to certain kinds of self-deception. It is sad that my parents, who were both admirable and loving, could through misunderstanding alone contribute to painful difficulties in their children's lives, even to fostering division among two daughters whose love for one another was of the deepest concern to them.

The last thing my mother said to me before she died was, "Love your sister." I passed it off at the time and repressed it later. Only now, through this unexpected prod to look at the importance of thumbsucking in early childhood, have I gained the insight to remember her injunction—even to begin to see why she felt this so necessary to say, and why it might be so fruitful for myself—again revealed as the Pharisee, but this time not by choice—to begin to try.

THE STORIES OF JESUS

Both as teacher and student, wrestling with the use of metaphor and meaning, I am reminded that Jesus told stories, too. All that we now have of the historical Jesus is the language he spoke and much of that is in parables. When I was young I heard of course the story of the sower sowing the seed and how some fell on thorny, some on rocky and some on barren ground. I kept hoping my heart was fertile for the word of the Lord. But what did I think that word was? The parables were so heavily moralized to us, it seemed then that the word merged with passive obedience, fidelity to rules and laws of the Church—with being "good" or at least repenting and then trying to resist temptation.

Now that I have learned something about texts, I know that one must often rescue the real one in order to grasp its message. In his remarkably concise book that I have already mentioned, John Dominic Crossan helps us gain a vivid sense of a different message from the Parables than the one I received as a child. In so doing, he also deals with many of the puzzles I've had with them over the years: Why is it the one in need who is the neighbor in the story of the Good Samaritan, for example, rather than the one who helps him? Most of these puzzles, it seems, have developed through changes and additions by the different authors who had—like my nuns—their own moral aims. Crossan's masterful job of uncovering these accretions suggests that Jesus did not share their purposes; he never gave specific moral advice.

Jesus could tell even the shocking story of the Wicked Husbandmen who succeed in beating the absent landlord's servants and killing his son, or the less terrible but still jarring account of the unjust servant, praising him for making friends for himself by forgiving others his master's debts. Have we not wondered, too, about the justice done the laborers who worked all day in the vineyard and received the same wages as those who came in at the eleventh hour, not to mention the short shrift given the Prodigal Son's older brother?

We have been worrying, Crossan says, because we thought these stories were pieces of moral advice. But to Jesus they were an expression of his experience of the Kingdom of God. Because the Church had his life for a model as well as his stories, we received that expression through constant reinterpretation. "The truth always lies in the interpretation," Raimundo Panikkar said once, eyes flashing with delight at the double meaning in his verb. Is there no way, then, that we might uncover what Jesus himself meant?

Despite all the difference in time, culture and

language, Crossan says that to some extent, we can. We must first understand that Jesus speaks as a poet in these stories: He teaches in symbols, not mere allegories, because he is not seeking to convey information, to give moral instruction, but to convey a new view of life. One must participate in the symbol in order to see.

His expression matches his experience of the Kingdom of God, the main and continuing burden of his parables, and in his vision that is an *action* in the present. All the parables that deal with finding treasure, or the pearl of great price, or even the lost sheep and the coin are speaking of the advent of new being the Kingdom brings. Finding it, one sells what one has (or leaves it) to gain the desired new life. Jesus is telling us that our world will be shaken, our values changed, indeed *reversed* by the entrance of God's world. He illustrates that reversal in the story of the "good" Samaritan in which the priests are "bad". The first becomes last and the last becomes first; the stone that was rejected becomes the cornerstone. The invisible social and linguistic structures that ruled Israel at that time, even the Pharisaic, which was highly demanding, is shattered by God's arrival in that world. Jesus illustrates this powerful surprise in stories that call on us to respond to our own life in a new way.

But why parables? Well, what other way *is*

there to make an auditor feel a world turned topsy-turvy? There is no simple linear way to involve a hearer in the kind of change hearing the Lord's voice means; it asks for a personally created response to a new kind of call. The vision of polar reversal in a parable may at least suggest this meaning to those capable of hearing, as Jesus himself said. What is good about Crossan's book is that he makes much current scholarship available around the crucial nature of the message of Jesus, but he does not try to answer unanswerable questions. Laying the stories bare as he can in the way he believes Jesus told them he leaves us to face the perennially new mystery ourselves.

SLUMPING IN CHURCH

Going to mass today in a small city on one of New York state's Finger Lakes, I slumped as usual as soon as I was forced to my knees. But today, from my conscious middle-aged viewpoint, especially after having reconsidered thumbsucking, I cannot just assume this bodily posture without wondering about it, too.

I looked at the unpretentious crowd in summer dresses and shirtsleeves around me. Many with venerable gray heads were also slumped over the pews. Very few ramrods around, no hats at all (curious, unremarked and almost spontaneous occurrence) and I felt no guilt as I would have when we assembled as a group in St. Sebastian's under the watchful eye of Sr. St. John of the Cross or Mother Grace.

Was I merely reacting against external prohibition? I defended myself instinctively; I have back problems and I can *pray* better this way. Even when I was a shepar ded child I wasn't *only* trying to be more comfortable; being relaxed I could think better about receiving Jesus within myself—I could concentrate and make the spiritual presence more real in my mind so he would truly cleanse my heart and help me live more honestly and kindly with others.

But is this what I'm doing now? No; frankly,

like everyone else, I'm just more relaxed in church than I used to be. Yet we are participating in a highly formal ritual. In theory it would seem that we should be kneeling straight—if only for the style and appropriateness. The emphasis here is on public act and not on private consciousness. We did not even have a homily this morning, so the shared ritual bore all the burden of our worship.

I remember Sister St. John sitting behind us as we used to go in graduated rows to the communion rail, eyes downcast and hands clasped. How well I knew such externals were unrelated to interior attitude; you could be thinking of movie stars and look like an angel. The only way to show true reverence then seemed to be by daring to slump, knowing that concentrated prayer was more important than external form. Such paradoxes in our behavior then. I greatly feared chewing the host as if I might be hurting the body of Jesus. I never thought how silly the apostles would look if they hadn't chewed the bread Jesus gave them at the Last Supper.

Yet here I am automatically slumping as if I had just escaped Sister last year! I reluctantly admit there is a *point* to kneeling straight during the mass—if we are aware of what we are doing, that position is not only suitable but should be desired physically as well as formally.

Mary Douglas says the child in the middle-class home is brought up to neglect the symbolic value of communication because all the emphasis is placed on *interior* intention. But at what a loss! I cannot help but believe in ritual, from bedtime stories to baseball games. The form and the rules are important, regardless of inner feelings, for there are social reasons for their existence. They are public channels and signs of emotional participation.

Yet here I am at mass, worshipping publicly, yet slumping, although I am here in and through my body to receive the body of the Lord as sign and sacrament that his church still tries to bring about his Kingdom in myself and in the world. If I were *really* here, I would be willingly, spontaneously reverent in posture as in thought. Oh Sister St. John, if only you had taught me yoga instead of saying, "Don't slump!" But why should I make you responsible for me? I might have resisted that, too. See how long it has taken me even to be aware of the stubborn childishness of my own public behavior.

CHANGING ATTITUDES TO PERSON

Driving back and forth to class, the market or the cleaners, I have almost automatically tuned in the radio news (that American habit of not wanting to waste a minute). Trying to gird myself physically and intellectually to do a paper on "person" for my class in human development seems not only difficult in our current atmosphere, but almost irrelevant. Whatever political reasons are given, large decisions which implicate and claim to represent all of us are based on quite impersonal forces: The decision of the government or the military to continue as No. One Strong Man (the old "fastest gun in the West" syndrome still dominates the American imagination) and the decision of the economic power-trust to let people suffer rather than look closely at what banks do or challenge the reign of the price structure in our society.

One is reminded that it would have been a disgrace for a man in the Nixon administration to have seen a psychiatrist, even in the face of evidence that indicates how much such help was needed. Little seems to have been learned in governing circles since. How helpless and ineffectual one feels, then, when experience, as well as the knowledge and insight gleaned from reading, indicate that the "personal" matters so slighted are nevertheless of the utmost importance.

My *conscious* awareness of the significance of being a person probably developed some ten years ago when I began to interview Catholic women about their hopes and problems. I had naturally always assumed and enjoyed the priority of "personal" attachments, the value of "personal" choice, the uniqueness of "personal" talent; such things gave the fabric of life its tough weave and its rich design. But when I considered my situation as a member of a church beginning to refer to itself as "the people of God" and began to ask other women how they felt as its members, I discovered a curiously common thread of response. The Catholic women I heard from—nuns, single women, married women of all ages—almost all felt as if they had been urged to fill roles, meet ideals, live up to expectations—Pius XI's "heart of the home," Pius XII's "spiritual motherhood" and the omnipresent "complement of man" stated as recently as April 18, 1975 by Paul VI. Many were being torn apart by the tension between the actual demands their life-situations made on them and the ideals which seemed impossible to live up to, but made them feel guilty when they did not. The women who were beginning to put themselves together (on the basis of knowledge from their experience) spoke of their own responsibility for their ideals as well as their behavior. They were beginning to call for recognition as full "persons" with the accompanying right to make decisions based on their sense of responsibility as independent adults. Most of these women were quite willing to give up the praise of "pedestalism" in order to share the real work of the world on an equal basis. As Sister Mary Luke Tobin, the one official American woman auditor at the second Vatican Council had observed, "The Church has always upheld the dignity of woman, now it must see her equality. We've been entirely too passive. What is needed now is theology of equality, and it must have its roots in a context of total reality."

This meant not only an inner struggle for the women involved, but also an outer struggle for public expression and for political advancement to make such changes socially acceptable. Yet the very "personal" qualities praised in women had been private virtues. It was difficult for them to break into an arena where in fact these "personal" values were not valued. Let us not delude ourselves, says Peter Berger in *Invitation to Sociology: A Humanistic Perspective,* the church as we mostly encounter it is basically a bureaucracy. And some women eager to win an equal share in it have begun to undervalue (or to relegate to their private lives) the very personal qualities others were struggling to affirm against its impersonality. One nun I know described all the years of her order's attempt to redesign its lifestyle according to Vatican II guidelines as an attempt "to make our own, to live internally" what before had been intellectual precepts, rules and external patterns. In pain and growing perception, this woman had come alive in middle age with new sensitivity to others, now choosing and selecting how to live a Christian vocation that before had been largely imposed, even though it implied internal consent.

Another nun, however, was scornful even of the language used by the first sister, who had spoken of the extreme importance of respecting the feelings of older sisters and of making each choice a "personal" one. "That won't help the sisters; I know them. What they need is to organize and pressure the hierarchy for the power they deserve. We have to leave that personal stuff behind."

This sister had an eye for political reality, and there is no doubt that many Catholic women needed her vision, too. Obviously the word "personal" is being used in many different ways, not always positive, depending on the way women are moving, but even those like this nun-organizer, who scorns values that have kept her group down, (on a sub-personal level) are part of understandable patterns. Our culture had relegated women largely to the private world where they were to be the guardians of the virtues of caring, nourishing, waiting, about which they were to remind the larger world from time to time. Cut off from the public daily sphere where important decisions were being made, (impersonally, of course), they also developed silly and often sick (or childish) manifestations, sending flowery cards on feast-days and anniversaries, dressing like "ladies" and speaking with carefully modulated voices.

But something powerful existed in the concept and the dawning experience of "personhood" that went far beyond such manifestations. Especially among those thoughtful women who seemed to be adapting to this realistic world while they also preserved a continuity with the selves they had been and now were, more consciously, choosing and creating. I picked up by chance a recent document put out by the Center of Concern in Washington, an influential group of independent Catholics—priests, nuns, and laity (three out of four writers of this paper are women). This statement on "Women in Church and Society" is a critique on the UN Feb. '75 draft of the International Women's Year World Plan of Action. They made comments on its inadequacies, and suggested as their first addition:

1) *Woman is a Full Person.* The plan of Action fails to state unequivocally that woman *as person* is the only acceptable definition upon

which all additional statements and considerations in the Plan must be built.

The age-old practice of viewing woman solely in terms of her child-bearing, child-rearing functions—a practice that has denied her the opportunity to develop the full range of her potential and has denied society the riches of her full personhood—must be forever laid to rest. It is time to end defining women, and thus limiting her, by biology. The Plan clearly lacks this primacy of personhood as a fundamental basis upon which any further definition of woman must be built.

Women like those writing this statement are unwilling to give up commitments to social and political justice; they intend to work for full equality legally and economically, but they are convinced that there is a *connection* between such visionary goals and the deep respect and tolerance that must be given to all individuals as they try to grow and learn to be themselves in a world all too ready to type them as "underprivileged," "middle-aged," "blue collar," "cop" or "long-hair". And so it would seem that this problem of the importance of the person is not only a weak and womanly need, but may well represent an historical sharing by women in a psychological and sociological process that is important to the evolution of what a strongly personal Pope, John XXIII, would refer to as the human family.

When I was a child, I had thought of "persons" as finished and unchangeable, though often obviously unpredictable. That was part of their "character," and I spent seemingly endless hours trying to figure out the puzzling and difficult characters of those I had to deal with—such as sisters, teachers and parents. I also tried to figure out what my "character" was like. Only much later and with some difficulty did I begin to sort out what seemed to be "given" and what I might change. Even this awareness, however, was at a superficial level, and my private world of fantasy was inadequately related to the physical me that went to class, acted in plays and dreamed of glory.

The years alone brought a slow but irreversible understanding of the process of growth and its importance in creating a person who in fact could develop, in time, and even relate some of her deepest inner hopes to an outward stance or a way of bringing up children. But mostly the effort seemed chaotic, still very split between private and public in the hectic world of parenting.

About this time I read the French philosopher Emmanuel Mounier's *Personalism,* with its clear division between "individual," that number recorded by the state which owns things and takes part in all sorts of legal and acquisitive transactions, and the "person," the living being who is born and dies and is subject to the vicissitudes of life. Pope John's call in *Pacem in Terris* for all human persons to build the earth together was also inspiring as an ideal, a vision of what we should be doing. And finally the insights psychology offers seemed most helpful to me in combining the idea, the ideal and the real in one's own life. I came to psychology late and hesitatingly, largely through religion. Literature had been my main teacher earlier on the intricacies of the human psyche. But one need not apply literature to one's life, whereas in psychology that is the whole point. The processive nature of human growth, its precariousness at each stage of development, the continual interaction between the individual and the environment in this process, and the difficulty of becoming a mature person became forcefully and permanently a part of my outlook. It has helped me to connect the various parts of my life into a more unified whole.

I also learned from psychology how important feelings are in coloring perception, and hence in influencing both our understanding and our behavior. The painful, isolated groping that so many women have been undergoing is seen to be quite natural and human in a culture that tends to downplay feeling except as it can be in some way manipulated for someone else's purpose. I say "natural" first because not all human growth is personal, at least not in the sense of being conscious. Very little is conscious, psychology tells us, and that's just the way we are. To be human is to acknowledge and live with this reality gracefully. "So often intellect mops up the floor with feelings" said my psychology teacher, Dr. Bell. Some women who have been pioneers in professional groups of men have experienced this personally. The feelings not expressed or considered important often are far more significant in the group than the words spoken; frequently they conflict. But women who have struggled with this situation personally, and who are *aware* of what is going on, are able to live in this atmosphere, and possibly to help put its ideas more in tune with the actual feelings of others present. I am not saying this is "woman's nature"; it merely seems that those who have undergone this struggle may be more sensitive to the process in others. "If feelings get shared, thoughts will get sorted out" said Dr. Bell, not the other way round.

And so the difficult struggle many women have had, to learn responsibility for themselves despite social expectations and church teachings that often seemed to define their very existence in terms of others was part of their becoming mature human beings. There was even a relation between writing the paper on "person" and my helpless feeling in the car listening to "impersonal" decisions of state. Because the reasons given for these decisions were not straightforward—they reflected either dishonesty or, more likely, lack of understanding of the real sources of their existence. And a feeling of weakness should not make one give up appreciation of personal values despite their vulnerability, for unless and until these values can become a part of the public sphere, neither private lives nor public policy can be maturely human.

THE PAPACY AND HOUSEWIFERY

Today's sermon, on the feast of Saints Peter and Paul, concerned the papacy, and how unfortunate it is that the institution that once served to unify Christians should now serve to divide them. Yet the Pope is serving a necessary caretaker's job, the priest insisted, presiding over vastly different worldwide groups of people who were not ready in reality for the future vision of the church John XXIII had given them. The legacy is there, but meanwhile many internal matters need to be attended to, before one day again, the Bishop of Rome might be seen primarily as the unifying religious leader of humankind.

The temptations for popes and housewives are much the same, it seems. Keeping things from rust and the moth is a full-time job, and someone has to be responsible. Any housewife knows that unless you keep up with it, everything gets out of control. Deterioration sets in, then hopelessness follows and human morale is lowered.

In the more complicated webs of human relations, however, mothers and popes seem to have even more in common. Both exist to nourish and nurture their children; both aim at fostering that combination of vision and responsibility in their charges that will enable them to become adults who will not need such care, and may be able to give it to others.

But being constantly inside one place, whether it is home or the Vatican, also tends to make the occupant more aware of all the inside work that needs doing rather than of the needs of those in the wide world outside. One who has peeled with the paint, suffered with the rot and mildew and grown furious with clutter knows very well how such struggles can stretch out and make one lose a sense of proportion about people's feelings and world events. A mother who has been too absorbed to notice that her adolescent son has gained a new sense of sophistication in the month since she last looked closely may be surprised by the way he shrinks in public, embarrassed, at a possessive word from her. After this experience, she can perhaps understand very well how an occupant of the Vatican might get out of touch with the world-related needs of his global family.

No doubt John XXIII's grasp of this tendency explains why he opened the windows when the stunned cardinals asked him why he was calling a council in the first place. But transforming the naturally overprotective attitude of housewife or pope is not only a matter of letting the fresh air in. John's gesture symbolized much more. Perhaps if he had been on the ground floor and been able to open the door we might have come closer to his meaning.

CRASH

The first few days of summer, so hazy and hot that you can smell the East River in the city, the honeysuckle out here, and see hope on faces seeking bargains in the thrift shops or playing tennis passionately on the public courts. But there is still a common sense of waiting and doubting if the recession is over. The news beams its double-bind message of gas shortages and higher prices, while the smiling President says it's all behind us. We just have to understand that things will *continue to improve* if we will only pay higher prices. Pass the Fresca.

Suddenly the smooth young man who's made it to the network anchor position changes his expression. "A 727 jetliner carrying 115 persons has crashed on a boulevard just outside Kennedy airport. We don't know yet how many survivors there are or what the cause was. Some bystanders claim the tail of the plane was struck by lightning."

I put down the Fresca. He refuses to read some trivial news items; a human being hides beneath that custom face. As the broken reports of disaster trickle in, the combined fascination and repulsion of both of us, newscaster and viewer, make it clear that we are witnessing our modern dance of death. The skeleton we have repressed through all the White House reports, the movie and restaurant reviews, flashes obscenely across the screen and we know the utter truth of the horror: it could have happened to any one of us. It *will* happen one way or another. So we follow the burned bodies to the hospital, the morgue; we pray for the two little girls who are less badly burned than their father, though their mother is probably dead. Nobody knows for sure what happened to the plane, but at least 109 people are dead. All night long, cleaning the dishes, reading, watering the tomato plants, feelings come and go: the natural good June feeling, remembering, and then relief that it wasn't me, forgetting again, watching the Mets win their first game in a week with Koosman in top form, then guilt at feeling so good as the hospital reports come on between the innings—forgetting again, and sleep.

The next morning the *Times* makes it official:

First big crash here since '65.
Four Prominent Persons among Passengers.
Two Children survive.

say the headlines. Our American mores are startlingly clear in reaction to disaster. A bishop and a basketball player are more prominent even in death. The plane crash is our Wheel of Fortune, then, as well as our Dance of Death. Those who go high are punished for their presumption; old superstitions abound. We cheer for the children, however; they carry all our hopes, even though we know that in six months, when their need will be so much greater, we will have completely forgotten them.

A disaster shatters our insulation. It releases us from the everyday grind; it pulls us together forcibly for the kind of emotional communion we so seldom feel. Writing *Mrs. Dalloway,* Virginia Woolf had the vision to see that a plane flying over London unified, for a brief moment, all those within earshot on the streets below, and she used the fact to relate a shellshocked young veteran to her middle-aged heroine. In our time it takes a crash to have us share the same emotions.

Not that most of us know what to do with the reality. The newspaper details the sad story of policemen threading their way through the scattered debris in the mud looking for life and not finding it, chatting nervously with bystanders who are attracted like ants to honey, accepting sandwiches from well-wishers. Thousands of teen-agers stream in on bicycles and motorcycles but soon get bored and leave. Priests say the last rites and everyone makes small talk, feeling no doubt a complete disjunction between the immensity of their inadequacy and the charred heaps of human jetsam.

No, we are almost totally unprepared on how to cope with this reality. Except with police cars and emergency measures in the hospital. In a few days those of us who are not personally involved will probably further repress the dancing skeleton. For what would happen if we did not, and met the next crash with no surprise, but with receptive observation, carefully assessing its damages in terms of physical suffering and longterm psychological damage? We might feel compelled either to change some of our attitudes to technology and its importance in our society, or feel challenged to become saints, people who could walk out compassionately amid the wreckage knowing the crash was not the complete interruption of our lives it seemed back in the living room, but rather an incendiary yet precise statement of our position in the society in which we live.

Months later people still recall the crash with shaking heads and hushed, serious tones, as if at the funeral of friends. Media dissemination of such disasters serves the reflective Christian today as the skull did on the desk of the late medieval philosopher. Truly it is our dance of death.

DEATH IN DAILY LIFE

Woke up thinking about how important it is to realize that death is coming to each of us, but how freighted with fearful emotional and mental preparation that word "realize" is. I remember our pastor advised us once during the Lenten season to write our own epitaphs: a sobering and constructive assignment, for it not only reminds us of the limited time ahead, but motivates us towards using it so that we might say something worthwhile that could still be true.

One of my favorite figures of speech is Benjamin Franklin's epitaph, written "in his own hand writing" in 1776:

The Body of
B. Franklin, Printer
Like the Cover of an Old Book
Its Contents torn out
And stript of its Lettering and Gilding,
Lies here, Food for Worms.
But the Work shall not be lost;
For it will, as he believe'd, appear once more
In a new and more elegant Edition
Corrected and improved
By the Author.

The fun and faith of this highly pragmatic American shine through his appropriately chosen simile. Pope John used figurative language, too, trying to cheer up the somber watchers at his own deathbed. "I am ready to take the great journey," he reassured them smiling weakly. "My trunks are packed." Never was the spiritual intent clearer than in his reference to luggage, for Angelo Roncalli's earthly goods, which had never been great, had gone already to his family to help them buy back the family home. He owned only the fountain pen by his bedside in his last illness, and this he gave in gratitude to his doctor, begging him, "Please take it. It's almost new. I've hardly used it."

Quite honestly, I don't yet feel up to writing my epitaph, though I may well ask my students to write theirs and see what happens. Another remark Pope John made on his eighty-first birthday, before he was dying, seems more fruitful to me now. "Every day is a good one to be born on" he observed, "and every day is a good one to die on." This matter-of-fact acceptance of death as an ordinary part of life is not natural to me, intent on my plans for the day and interested in other people. Despite the fact that I read Tolstoy's "The Death of Ivan Ilyich" yearly with my class, I continue to find myself more like the characters in the early part of the story who deny that Ivan's death had anything to do with them, except as they fret about missed card games (because of the wake) and speculate on who will get the dead man's job.

Maybe there is some carryover. As I fried eggs and bacon this morning I thought of the chicken and the pig who contributed to our continuance with their involuntary sacrifice, and I thanked them. This belated gratitude is not nearly on the spiritual level of the Indians who used to pray before the hunt to the spirit of the deer they hoped to kill, assuring it they hunted only because of need, and promising it they would waste no part of him, neither hide nor hoof. When I was younger, however, I would never have considered hen and pig as kindred.

The natural connection between death and the daily sustenance of life brought to my mind quite suddenly a series of personal encounters with close relatives in which each seemed to show a premonition of oncoming death by an intense natural desire, involving physical change, yet clearly bearing symbolic value that transcended it. My father wished to move to a house by the ocean, telling us he longed to look out over it. Although he had loved sea stories and greatly admired Columbus and other hardy navigators, his desire was a surprise to us, and I thought back on it only when he died in the very process of moving. A few years later, my mother told me she was yearning to visit the White Mountains, a place we had not visited together since I was five, but which had been for me then, as for her, a revelation of nature's vast, impersonal glory, quite unlike the tame Rhode Island scenery. She grew fatally ill so rapidly we could not make the trip.

And finally Aunt Geraldine, my delightful singing aunt who seemed healthy when I saw her, told me of her dream the night before: She saw my mother and Gaga and Aunt Ann walking arm in arm over the crest of a hill in the sunshine, smiling and waving to her to join them. The dream had greatly comforted her. I remembered it three months later when she died "unexpectedly" of a heart attack.

On a simpler level of life, the flower and the vegetable spring from the compost heap of decaying matter. Again the necessary corruption. Reflection should convince us humans that we are the very tip of life proceeding from the rich genetic and evolutionary compost heap of those beings who have struggled and died to produce this vulnerable growth. To say that life is a part of death might be almost more exact than the reverse. My own memories and the wisdom of a John XXIII suggest that far from being morbid, such an awareness leads us to a sense of our grateful communion with created nature and our forebears as well as to a freer, more creative attitude to the brief growth we have to nourish.

JUGGLING

Two books I have read recently have had a considerable effect on reorienting my ideas about space-time, and may make a difference in how I teach. The first is *Hidden Injuries of Class* by American sociologists Richard Sennett and Jonathan Cobb (Knopf, 1972) and the second is *Natural Symbols* by English anthropologist Mary Douglas (Vintage Books, 1973).

Interviewing ethnic workers in the Boston area, Sennett and Cobb came up with findings that are admittedly subtle and highly interpretative, yet make sense out of otherwise puzzling contradictions. The workers shattered the stereotype of materialistic, law-and-order patriarchs because—despite the behavioral psychologist's denial of such values—they sought primarily the elusive goals of personal freedom and dignity. But because of the dominant American economic and social structures, they had been taught since kindergarten that these rewards would come only to those who left the communal support of lower-class factory work, got "educated," and forged into the competitive field of paper-pushing jobs. Thus a loss of self-respect as well as group rapport was built in to the process of upward social mobility. Since nagging doubts about the value of self-worth accompanied the middle-class job, even when the material rewards were real, the worker did not feel that he had made something of himself as he had hoped. In turn, the worker would place these frustrated hopes on his children's future, thus putting impossible strains on family life and usually guaranteeing future estrangement from his pressured children. For the ethnic worker, this painful progression towards material gain with its consequent spiritual and psychological loss was not made out of desire to consume and own things, but rather to take the path our society points out—with emphasis—as the only one for achieving personal freedom and dignity.

Mary Douglas suggests other usually invisible differences between working and middle-class mores that cause much misunderstanding between them and lead to unfair generalizations. Summarizing recent linguistic discoveries, she points to the different use of language in different classes. Working-class children are raised by their families and later taught in their schools to grasp language as a reinforcement of a hierarchical and spatially organized universe. To children asking "Why?" the usual answers are: "Because that's the way it is," "Because I say so," or "Because you're a boy." In this restricted language, speech is not a vehicle of communication on an interpersonal level. Schools which emphasize "right answers" confirm this tendency. Visual and oral symbols, however, tend to take on considerable communicative power since they are vehicles commonly understood, and the response to them is intensely emotional.

Middle-class children have a very different introduction to language. From the first time they ask, "Why can't you play with me?" and are told, "I'm tired now, but I will after tea," they learn that speech is for personal communication. Status and reasons are almost as elastic as the person talking, and language can be a means of self-expression and a way to reach out to others. The point of the difference is made clear when Mary Douglas cites the discomfiture of the Bog Irish (from whom she claims descent) with the post-Vatican II demotion of the long-held Catholic abstinence from meat on Friday in deference to the socially acceptable middle-class view of the primary importance of an interior, personal commitment to abstinence.

Our very way of talking, then, even when we speak the same language, may nevertheless indicate that we live in differently perceived worlds, even when only blocks apart. The findings in these books help me understand, for instance, the resentment certain students show in college. The hidden injury of class reveals itself when some young man or woman, present because of parental will, shows automatic annoyance at any authority. "I don't care what Dostoevsky *thought* he was writing. That's my opinion of what he *said.*" Older students will have more deferential attitudes towards authority, even an inflated idea of what schooling may offer, but they will also resist notions that conflict with their own ordered conceptions: *"That* is not poetry. It has no rhyme, no meter and no message!"

How often in the past I've argued about such things. Yet now I feel I was merely using verbal language (part of the distrusted culture) to shape into line people whose quarrel was with society and their own upbringing. Can the classroom allow us to share different cultural conceptions and work out common answers to such basic questions as, "What is a poem? How valid is *my* impression of it? What relation do stories and poems have to truth, anyway?"

I have seen the classroom space come alive when recognition is made and acceptance given to the many invisible marks the past has made on the individuals sitting there. As a sense of each other's differentness grows among them, students show a remarkable delicacy and unanimity in supporting each other. Last year I had a red-headed, fiercely blue-eyed grandmother in class whose hand would tremble as she tried to get out a few words about a story she'd liked. Slowly we learned bits of her childhood as an orphan in Brooklyn, and particularly her fascination with one attractive and independent aunt on whom stylish and cultured gentlemen would call while little Mary sat enthralled at the dining room table. Her taste in literature was flawless; she thirsted for the most profound and subtle writing that often tested the patience of the other students. As their respect and encouragement grew, however, Mary's nervousness became so intense it was almost incoherent. Finally she broke down in class and confided to us that her husband and her 27-year-old son had told her she should quit college.

"I brought them all up. How much house-keeping can you do?" she asked us. We told her to tell them how much it meant to her to come. She tried, and the family seemed to understand. Mary began to write a little as well as cut in on the conversation with a fiery faithfulness if she felt someone was unfair to Faulkner or Fitzgerald. A few months later, however, the old nervousness returned. She came up after class to explain why she was so distracted. "Pop," as she called her husband, had received a promotion; last night he had brought home a big box containing a mink coat and diamond earrings. "Now," he begged her, "will you quit college?"

She felt twisted inside, torn between the person she loved and a deep and inexplicable urge for learning. With a little help from some of the class, Mary and Pop again reached some kind of understanding. She tried hard to tell him that her love of college had nothing to do with any lack of love for him or any inadequacy as a husband on his part.

These people are struggling like so many others, against the hidden injuries—the goals, the roles—society inflicted on them while pursuing its institutional objectives. Struggling is something; knowing what forces we wrestle with is something more. And now, as adults, we are taking the opportunity to meet others who can expand our vocabularies and our vision, who can even help us find clues to strengths and weaknesses in ourselves we had not known of.

The excitement and energy that can be generated in a classroom is new to me. The classrooms I remember as a child rewarded decorum and memory, tracing instead of drawing. Those spaces were thick with expectations, competition, fears of failure. I was amazed not too long ago to visit my old home and grammar school after having been away some twenty-five years. Physically the buildings seemed the same, but it was like seeing a town in a dream. The space between the buildings looked empty, free to let me fit in joy at returning and pleasure in the newly-appreciated architecture. I could not see or feel all the powerful pressures that undoubtedly still filled that town for the people who were growing up there now or had never gone away.

But I knew now that those spaces were not empty. The reason I knew it was because of my son's interest in juggling. Slumped in a chair one night during one of his infrequent visits, I had watched him throwing three and four oranges in the air, catching them in ever wider circles, joking, throwing one to me and getting me to throw it back, never missing a beat, body relaxed and eyes attentive, moving, spreading infectious happiness.

He showed me that juggling doesn't work if you think too much about it or feel you have to steel yourself for a special, limited effort. Instead, it involves complete relaxation and attention to where you are. To be prepared to last, you've got to believe anything's possible, relax, swing the arms freely and concentrate with the eyes. "Just *throw* the balls," Peter said. "You don't have to catch them, just throw them." Then you can perform feats that look as if they defy the laws of motion. You find you do catch them. Getting the third ball up for the first time—the one that's in the air when you're handling the others—is such a surprise the amateur gasps, tightens up, and the ball thuds to the floor. But try it again and again, accept the extraordinary flight as natural and, miraculously, you can keep it up.

After that experience, any space looks more alive with possibility than it did before. Now I wonder that it took me so long to see that my very idea of space had become deadened by the hidden injury I suffered, feeling I had to get away from authority to some sort of empty place. The classroom is my juggling place now, and the bats and Indian clubs come from all directions. But I think more and more of us are finding our own places, feeling that at least we're playing a game that might give us some sort of mastery that is satisfying. At least it's a space with potential.

...TODAY WILL BE YESTERDAY

When I began this exploration I think I understood my father's childish observation on time pretty much as he did. He had a scientific bent, so I suppose the discovery for him was like finding out how a clock works. For me, however, the big clock carried dark psychic undertones. When tomorrow comes, today will be yesterday and so time goes on, relentlessly, to dusty death. Memory having reawakened my curiosity to look more intently at yesterday, however, I find I now have a different understanding of his remark. Rethinking (and even redreaming) the past has yielded new meaning to me today about past and present relations with many intimate friends and taught me that "today will be yesterday" can be a moveable term. Of course today turns into yesterday, but yesterday can also revisit today and charge it with new meaning that offers possibility for the future.

This recognition gives me a different attitude to the time-game I play when appointments are cancelled and unexpected choices are possible. The difference lies, I suspect, in my changed attitude to time and space. I used to think that space was empty, and that the pressure of time urged me to fill it up. Reflecting during this introspective year, I have come to see that my concept of space was wrong because I had not included time and motion within it. Watching my son juggling, I learned that time is not the enemy and that empty space is an illusion, an error that leads to the death of hope.

I see the space around me now permeated by yesterday—that round table inlaid with roses, for instance, snatched from the family home minutes before the new purchaser arrived, will always bear for me some of my mother's gentility. I see people, too, moved by their own past so that often they react to that instead of to what we are talking about now. I do it too; I snap at my husband and realize almost instantly that I am reacting to a parent or a sister telling me what to do.

The vital invisible effects of other times and places affect our present social lives as well. Why do the Haitians among my students keep separate from the others? Although physically they are in the same town, they live in a different world, one filled with a proud, exotic history and the fierce struggle to survive with dignity. Sight of the eyes alone does not reveal the enormous differences that exist among a group of people who may look and dress alike, yet who hold a set of assumptions and memories others do not dream of, let alone share.

Not until the last meeting of a class section a year ago did a Haitian student tell us about the time when as a child he had seen men under a curse turn into pigs. The other students rushed to say "You mean you *believe* you saw such a thing". Their shock and disbelief when he said calmly, "I saw it," was tempered by the enormous respect the class had developed for the speaker's intelligence. Only in this last shared time did we catch a glimpse of the powerful psychic forces alive and unsuspected in our own community.

The possibility of seeing more clearly the difference the past makes in the present also gives us greater opportunity to deal with it realistically, so that we can affect our future through such perception. Knowing how different our neighbors are, and in what ways, we can approach them with fewer misconceptions, learn more from them about this complex humanity we share. Because we have learned how incredibly full the space-time around us already is, we need not be so anxious about filling up "free time" in a worthwhile way. If we think of an elderly neighbor in a free moment, what could be better than to make human contact immediately, even if briefly? And if we are, on the other hand, pressured by time so that we tend to become annoyed when others drop in on us, we have been working with false assumptions about time and people. Why not try a new tack with someone we've never been able to stand? We don't have to catch the balls; just throw them up and see. Maybe we can find some link; get them talking about their own childhood, discover a side we've never seen.

When we can see the circles in which we live and the lines between them on which we move so charged with inner meaning and possibility from the past and for the future, we are less likely to be bored or to exaggerate the importance of our own choices. Like Emily Dickinson who saw eternity so clearly in a single room, we can face our own existence more hopefully, knowing that growth and relationship from the many stories told and heard "in circuit," mediating "the truth's superb surprise," can fill our days. The sacred is all around us if we can learn to see and hear it in the roundabout way we must.

* * *

One of the common ways we can all catch glimpses of the truth in human guise is by re-visiting the lives of saints we admired as children. Bringing to them some of the wisdom as well as the puzzles adult life has given us, we may find deeper meaning in them today, just as we do in our personal memories. For me, a second look at Therese of Lisieux has been rewarding, and I should like to end by recounting one message this shortlived nineteenth-century French Carmelite sends to me. I choose her for two reasons: first, her story has been widely misconstrued, and second, she illustrates to an extraordinary degree the ability to improve one's perception of one's own space-time so that it can become, as the parables of Jesus suggest, an active vehicle of God's will.

Most of us learned of Therese when we were children, either through hearing the story of her "little way" to holiness through everyday trials or by seeing one of the innumerable statues of her, surrounded by the roses she was said to have promised to shed on those who would implore her help. Only in the 1950s when I learned that her two handwritten notebooks on her life and vocation, as well as her late photographs, had been reedited and retouched, was I curious enough to try to see what the original might have been like.

The headstrong, willful youngest daughter of a pious bourgeois family in the provinces came through this research much the same as in my childhood understanding. The great revelation of the unedited Therese was her growing understanding of her life's meaning. After a number of years in the convent she had stormed the authorities to enter, this devoted realist knew well how ordinary her spiritual life there was. It consisted of accepting the complaints and misunderstandings of the other sisters cheerfully, without attributing evil motives to them. It also meant accepting her own inability to keep her mind on her prayers, say the rosary while meditating, and still not let any of this shake her unalterable faith in God's power to work even through such ordinariness. Therese's increasingly realistic perception of convent life and of human weakness made her comments ironically humorous, but at the same time it increased her characteristic belief that God is anxious to love the world and that it is we who put up blocks and blinders.

Her unique vocation became clear to her in 1895 when she wrote about her seven years in the convent, under orders to do so from her Prioress sister, Pauline: "Thinking one day of those who offer themselves as victims to the justice of God, in order to turn aside the punishment reserved for sinners by taking it upon themselves, I felt this offering to be noble and generous, but was far from feeling myself drawn to make it." It should be noted that the ideal she did not accept was precisely that of the Lisieux Carmel. Young as she was, and eager to obey and serve the Carmelite rule in all things, her spirit had flowered far beyond its current limits. She objected to the "Noble sacrifice" because it posed the danger of thinking the just separate from sinners, and her own experience denied this separation. So did her understanding of God, who she saw as a loving God burning to break through the barriers sin erected against Him, not a just God anxious to punish. And so on the Feast of the Holy Trinity in 1895, Therese asked the Lord to accept her as a sacrifice to his love.

She was not surprised when on Good Friday of the following year, 1896, she discovered after undergoing a severe hemorrhage, that she had an advanced case of tuberculosis. She had expected suffering, but when on that Easter Sunday it was accompanied by doubts against the faith, she was forced to change somewhat her understanding of her vocation. The Lord made her feel "there really were souls who did not have faith. . . . He permitted my soul to be invaded by the most impenetrable darkness, and the thought of heaven, so sweet in my childhood, became nothing more than a source of struggle and torment." She now prayed in the name of "us poor sinners," saying she would eat the bread of sorrow at their table of bitterness till the end.

Her identification with sinners, so clear in her own words, was changed by the editors who substituted the word "unbelievers." There in the quiet convent of Lisieux, undergoing great pain until her death on Sept. 30, 1897, Therese persisted in believing in God's love as she lay surrounded by her real and spiritual sisters who saw only her goodness and sanctity. She wrote about her sisters' misunderstanding of her attitude in the second notebook before her last illness. Despite all her protestations, Celine and Pauline were to keep attributing saintly goodness and effectiveness to Therese, who felt only doubt and weakness, but *believed* in a loving God.

She spent her dying days wrestling with these sisters who tormented her with their "consolations" by outlining the heavenly bliss she was "earning". She reminded them just as constantly that Jesus died in agony. "I cannot be broken, tried, save by the just, for all my sisters are pleasing to God," she had written near the end. Perhaps we can understand a little of what she meant when we learn that Pauline would describe her death in the official published autobiography, *The Story of a Soul,* in the very language Therese had directly repudiated. Pauline spoke of those dying in "onslaughts of Love, in raptured ecstasies," while Therese had said: "I will be able to take no rest until the end of the world as long as there will be souls to save." It is in this context we must rethink the nature of the saint's roses.

Looking at unretouched photographs during her last illness and reading her own words, one has a vision of a tough-minded, stubborn and deeply charitable woman. The pencilled drawing we might make of the few circles and lines that would constitute the short time-space of her life reminds me poignantly of the truth of Berry's assertion that a single person, drawing deeply and honestly on her own resources, can see the richness possible in even so cramped a space, can find in faithful, clear-eyed service there, direct access to all reality. Therese is a modest and yet perfect example of how seeming isolation from others may well conceal deep sympathy and interrelationship with them.

To me, the story of Therese is one that helps solve the ultimate riddle of time-space, not by triumphing over or avoiding it, but by consenting to it fully in its most intense reality. She exemplified the rare vision philosopher Alfred North Whitehead held out as true wisdom: one that sees the forest through seeing the trees. Stripped of her pink plaster roses, Therese gives me courage. She even gives me hope that such realistic faith and wholehearted consent as hers may triumph over the limits of time and space in a way I cannot and need not now understand.